# IN ACTION

# Implementing Training Scorecards

EIGHT

CASE STUDIES

FROM THE

REAL WORLD

OF TRAINING

JACK J. PHILLIPS

SERIES EDITOR

LYNN SCHMIDT

EDITOR

ASTD

*Linking People,
Learning & Performance*

**ASTD Press** is an internationally renowned source of insightful and practical informati on workplace learning and performance topics, including training basics, evaluation and return-on-investment (ROI), instructional systems development (ISD), e-learning, leadership, and career development.

**Ordering Information:** Books published by ASTD Press can be purchased by visiting our Website at store.astd.org or by calling 800.628.2783 or 703.683.8100.

Library of Congress Catalog Card Number: 2002105504

ISBN: 1-56286-314-2

# Table of Contents

Introduction to the *In Action* Series ...............................................v

Preface.............................................................................vii

How to Use This Casebook .........................................................xi

The Value of Training Scorecards ..................................................1
Lynn Schmidt

Confronting a Future Crisis................................................13
Saint Elizabeth Health Care
Paul Hurly, Nancy Hawkes, and Kathy Craddock

Using Training Scorecards to Prove That Training Pays ..................41
Nextel Communications
Lynn Schmidt

Implementing Value Measurement: Return-on-Investment
   from Sprint University of Excellence ......................................65
Sprint
Joel S. Finlay

Six Levels of Training Evaluation: Improving Quality
   and Reducing Manufacturing Costs.......................................91
Analog Devices, Inc.
Mo Maghsoudnia and Lucy Strandberg

SQC Problem-Solving Training Program............................111
Toyota Industries Corporation
Uichi Tsutsumi and Susumu Kubota

The Competitive Weapon: Using ROI Measurement
   to Drive Results ..............................................................135
Large-Tech Corporation
*Theresa L. Seagraves*

Learning Services: Implementing a Training Scorecard
   to Demonstrate Value .......................................................161
The Mellear Corporation
*Stephanie Barber and Patricia Albaugh*

Caterpillar University Dashboard: Measuring—and Maximizing—
   the Business Value of Learning.........................................181
Caterpillar, Inc.
*Merrill C. Anderson and Chris Arvin*

About the Editor.......................................................................199

About the Series Editor ..........................................................201

# Introduction to the *In Action* Series

Like most professionals, the people involved in HRD are eager to see practical applications of models, techniques, theories, strategies, and issues relevant to their field. In recent years, practitioners have developed an intense desire to learn about firsthand experiences of organizations implementing HRD programs. To fill this critical void, the Publishing Review Committee of ASTD established the *In Action* casebook series. Covering a variety of topics in HRD, the series significantly adds to the current literature in the field.

The *In Action* series objectives are as follows:

- *To provide real-world examples of HRD program application and implementation.* Each case describes significant issues, events, actions, and activities. When possible, actual names of organizations and individuals are used. Where names are disguised, the events are factual.
- *To focus on challenging and difficult issues confronting the HRD field.* These cases explore areas where it is difficult to find information or where processes or techniques are not standardized or fully developed. Emerging issues critical to success also are explored.
- *To recognize the work of professionals in the HRD field by presenting best practices.* Each casebook represents the most effective examples available. Issue editors are experienced professionals, and topics are carefully selected to ensure that they represent important and timely issues. Cases are written by highly respected HRD practitioners, authors, researchers, and consultants. The authors focus on many high-profile organizations—names you will quickly recognize.
- *To serve as a self-teaching tool for people learning about the HRD field.* As a stand-alone reference, each volume is a practical learning tool that fully explores numerous topics and issues.
- *To present a medium for teaching groups about the practical aspects of HRD.* Each book is a useful supplement to general and specialized HRD

textbooks and serves as a discussion guide to enhance learning in formal and informal settings.

These cases will challenge and motivate you. The new insights you gain will serve as an impetus for positive change in your organization.

Jack J. Phillips
*In Action* Series Editor
P.O. Box 380637
Birmingham, AL 35238-0637
phone: 205.678.8038
fax: 205.678.0177
email: serieseditor@aol.com

# Preface

There is increasing pressure from stakeholders on training and development departments to show a return-on-investment. Many training and development departments struggle to align training programs with business strategies, but it can be difficult to find the best approaches to establish, track, collect, compile, analyze, and communicate training results. Many training and development departments don't know the results of the training programs they deliver, so they can't demonstrate the value they add to the business.

Through this casebook I hope to contribute to the understanding of training measurement and evaluation. The case authors, who reflect viewpoints from varied backgrounds, are all using training scorecards as a framework as they pursue training measurement and evaluation.

## Target Audience

This book should interest anyone involved in HR, HRD, or any type of training delivery. The primary audience is practitioners who are struggling to report the results of their training initiatives. They are the ones who request more real-word examples. This same group also expresses concern that there are too many models, methods, strategies, and theories, and too few examples showing that any of them has really made a difference. This publication should satisfy practitioners' needs by providing examples of how training scorecards have been implemented successfully.

The second audience comprises instructors and professors. Whether this casebook is used in university classes with students who are pursuing careers in training and development, at internal workshops for professional training staff, or at public seminars on training measurement and evaluation, it will be a valuable reference. It can be used as a supplement to a standard HRD or learning textbook or as a complement to a textbook on training measurement and evaluation. As a supplemental text, this casebook will bring practical significance to the coursework, convincing students that there are systematic processes, methods, and models that can help to measure and evaluate training initiatives.

A third audience is the managers who must work with these issues on a peripheral basis—those managers who are asked to spend their time and to offer the time of their employees to collect and analyze training data. These are managers who participate in training programs and ask other employees to participate, and who occasionally lead efforts in that area. In these roles, managers must understand the impact of training and appreciate the value of training solutions.

Each audience should find the casebook entertaining and engaging reading. Questions are placed at the end of each case to stimulate additional thought and discussion. One of the most effective ways to maximize the usefulness of this book is through group discussions using the questions to develop and dissect the issues, techniques, methodologies, and results.

## The Cases

The most difficult part of developing this book was to identify case authors who could contribute systems, processes, and models that provide a training scorecard approach to measuring and evaluating training initiatives. In the search, many people who had expressed interest in the topic of training scorecards were contacted—many of them outside the United States to tap the global market. I had more than 100 requests for guidelines to the casebook. Based on the response, I selected eight case studies to present here. These eight cases cover a variety of approaches and represent several industries, including health care, telecommunications, manufacturing, and high technology.

In my search for cases, I contacted the most respected and well-known organizations in the world, leading experts in the field, key executives, and well-known authors and researchers. I leave it to you to decide if best-practice cases were delivered. What I know is that if these are not best practices, no other publication can claim to have them either. Many of the experts producing these cases characterize them as the best examples of using training scorecards as a framework for measurement and evaluation.

Although some attempt was made to structure cases similarly, they are not identical in style and content. It is important for the reader to experience the solutions as they were developed and identify the issues pertinent to each particular setting and situation. The result is a variety of presentations with a number of styles. Some cases are brief and to the point, outlining precisely what happened and what was achieved. Others provide more background information, including details on how the people involved determined the need for the process, descriptions of the personalities involved, and analyses of how the backgrounds and biases of the people involved created a unique situation.

There was no attempt to restrict cases to a particular methodology, technique, or process. It is helpful to show a wide range of approaches. I resisted the temptation to pass judgment on various approaches, preferring to let the reader evaluate the techniques and their appropriateness in particular settings. Some of the assumptions, methodologies, and strategies might not be as comprehensive and sound as others.

## Case Authors

It would be difficult to find a more impressive group of contributors to a publication of this nature than those included here. I would describe the case authors as experienced, professional, knowledgeable, and on the leading edge of training measurement and evaluation. Most are experts, and some are well known in their fields. A few are high-profile authors who have made a tremendous contribution to the field and have taken the opportunity to provide an example of their top-quality work. Others have made their mark quietly and have achieved success for their organizations.

## Suggestions

As with any new publication, I welcome your input. If you have ideas or recommendations regarding presentation, case selection, or case quality, please send them to Lynn Schmidt, lynn.schmidt@nextel.com. These comments will be appreciated and acknowledged.

## Acknowledgments

I want to thank the case authors for their dedication and professional contributions to this book. It has been a pleasure working with them over the last several months. Their patience with the editing process has been greatly appreciated. There would be no book if the case authors had not been willing to share their stories. I also want to acknowledge the organizations that have allowed their names and solutions to be used for publication. I believe that the final product has portrayed them as progressive organizations interested in results and willing to try new processes and techniques.

I would also like to thank Jack Phillips, the series editor; Joyce Alff, the internal editorial director; and the American Society for Training & Development. I have enjoyed the process of creating this casebook and greatly appreciate the opportunity. It has been an incredible journey and an exceptional learning experience.

Lynn Schmidt
Ashburn, Virginia
January 2003

# How to Use This Casebook

The cases presented in this book illustrate various approaches to creating and implementing training scorecards. The cases focus on a number of methods that can be used to measure and evaluate training programs, including their return-on-investment. Collectively, the cases offer a range of settings, methods, techniques, strategies, and approaches. Moreover, they represent a wide spectrum of industries, including manufacturing, telecommunications, health care, and technology.

As a group, these cases are a rich source of information about the strategies of some of the best practitioners and consultants in the field. Yet, no case necessarily represents the ideal approach for the specific situation. In every case it is possible to identify areas that could benefit from refinement and improvement. That is part of the learning process—to build on the work of other people.

Table 1 presents basic descriptions of the cases in the order in which they appear in the book. It provides an overview of the cases by industry, focus areas, and training programs. It can serve as a quick reference for readers who want to examine the cases by particular audiences, industries, and case types.

## Using the Cases

There are several ways to use this book. Overall, it will be helpful to anyone interested in the topic of implementing training scorecards to compile and report training evaluation data, whether that person is a senior-level executive, an HRD/HR professional, or a measurement and evaluation consultant. Specifically, I recommend the following four uses:

1. Professionals can use this book as a basic reference of practical applications for training scorecards and their use in measuring and evaluating training programs. A reader can analyze and dissect each of the cases to develop an understanding of the issues, approaches, and, most of all, refinements or improvements that could be made.

# Figure 1. Overview of the case studies.

| Case | Industry | Focus of Case | Training Program(s) |
|---|---|---|---|
| Saint Elizabeth Health Care | Health care | Aligning a learning-and-development balanced scorecard with an HR balanced scorecard | Performance management and managing injured workers' training for managers of nursing staff |
| Nextel Communications | Telecommunications | Using a training scorecard to demonstrate the bottom-line impact of management development programs | Diversity awareness training for managers |
| Sprint | Telecommunications | Using value measurement summaries and project logs to report the bottom-line impact of performance improvement initiatives | New-hire training for call center accounts receivable representatives |
| Analog Devices, Inc. | High-technology manufacturing | Integrating a training scorecard with a production scorecard | Proficiency training focused on scrap reduction for inspectors and operators |
| Toyota Industries Corporation | Manufacturing | Using a training scorecard to report the impact of problem-solving skills on the bottom line | Statistical quality control training for engineers |
| Large-Tech Corporation | High technology hardware and software | Implementing a training scorecard to measure and report the bottom-line impact of sales training | Financial selling skills training for sales account executives and sales managers |

| Company | Industry | Topics |
|---|---|---|
| The Mellear Corporation | Telecommunication services | Lead-generation training for sales account executives |
| Caterpillar, Inc. | Construction equipment manufacturing | Creating a training scorecard to demonstrate the value of learning services initiatives<br>Using a training dashboard to report evaluation targets and the results of a variety of training programs<br>Leadership, manufacturing, technical, business, marketing, and Six Sigma training programs |

2. This book will be useful in group discussions during which interested individuals can react to the material, offer different perspectives, and draw conclusions about approaches and techniques.

3. This book can serve as an excellent supplement to other training and development textbooks. It provides the extra dimension of real-life cases that show the outcomes of using training scorecards to compile and report the results of training programs.

4. This book will be extremely valuable for managers and executives who do not have responsibility for compiling and reporting training data. These managers provide support and assistance to the HRD/HR staff, and it is helpful for them to understand the methodologies professionals use and the results that their solutions can yield.

Remember that each organization and its program implementation are unique. What works well for one may not work for another, even if both are in similar settings. The book offers a variety of approaches and provides many tools to assist with implementing a training scorecard.

## Follow-up

Space limitations have required that some cases be shorter than the author and editor would have liked. Some information concerning background, assumptions, strategies, and results had to be omitted. If additional information on a case is desired, please contact the lead author of the case or the book's editor. In most instances, the contact information for the lead author is provided in the biographical information following each case; the address of the editor is provided in the biographical information at the end of the book.

# The Value of Training Scorecards

Lynn Schmidt

*Webster's Unabridged Dictionary* (1998) defines "score" as the record of points or strokes made by competitors in a game or match; the act of making or earning a point or points; a tally. The same source defines "scorecard" as a card for keeping score of a sports contest. Imagine watching "Monday Night Football," attending a soccer game, playing tennis, or golfing without a scorecard for any of the games. No one knows the score or how the game is going. No one knows if the score is better or worse than the last game. The players, who have dedicated themselves to the sport and have invested a great deal of time and energy, don't know if they are playing as expected or if any improvements are needed. Individuals who either watch or participate in sports rely on the scorecard to know who is winning the game, how the competitors compare, and if improvements are required.

Businesses and organizations need to keep score as well. Imagine a training department that invests a lot of time and money in offering many training programs and development interventions but keeps no scorecard. No one knows how individuals are being affected. No one knows how the training department is doing. There is no information on whether the company is winning the game, how it compares with its competitors, and if improvements are needed. No one is asking the following questions:

- Are training participants satisfied?
- Is learning taking place?
- Has behavior changed?
- Are business results being affected?
- Is the company receiving a return on the investment being made?

Is the scenario as applied to a training department difficult or easy to imagine? Does your training organization have a scorecard?

According to ASTD's *State of the Industry* report for 2002, the number-one factor affecting the future of training and the workplace learning and performance field is money (Van Buren and Erskine, 2002). The increasing pressure from shareholders for realizing short-term profits prompts greater pressure on employees to produce results and on training to show a return-on-investment (ROI). But the data collected for the report indicates that not many companies have a training scorecard. Of the 367 benchmarking services companies included there, 78 percent measure satisfaction, 32 percent measure learning, 9 percent measure behavior change, and 7 percent measure business results. One could conclude from those percentages that many companies don't know their training department's score.

Jack Phillips (1999) conducted a research study on the top training and development trends worldwide. Here are the top six trends he identified:

1. Training and development costs are being monitored more accurately to manage resources and demonstrate accountability.
2. Measuring the return-on-investment in training and development is growing in use.
3. Systematic evaluation processes measure the success of training and development.
4. Needs assessment and analysis are receiving increased emphasis.
5. Training and development staff and line management are forming partnerships to achieve common goals.
6. Training and development is being linked to the strategic direction of the organization.

Immediate action will need to be taken by training departments to keep up with those trends. It will be important to improve continuously the techniques for keeping score in order to demonstrate the training department's ability to be a business partner and to add value to the business. The training scorecard is a tool that can help training departments determine if they are winning the game, how they compare with competitors, and if improvements are required.

## Business Scorecards

In 1990 the Nolan Norton Institute sponsored a study titled "Measuring Performance in the Organization of the Future" (Kaplan and Norton, 1996). David Norton served as the study leader and Robert Kaplan as an academic consultant. What prompted the study was the thought that current performance measurement approaches, primarily financial accounting, were becoming obsolete. Representatives from a dozen companies met for a year to develop a new performance measurement model. The outcome of this study was the "balanced scorecard." The balanced scorecard translates an organization's mission and strategy into a set of performance measures that provides a framework for a strategic measurement system. It emphasizes financial objectives but also includes the performance drivers of those objectives. The scorecard measures organizational performance from four perspectives: financial, customer, internal business processes, and learning and growth.

In the 11 years since the study was completed, it is reported that 50 percent of organizations in North America and western Europe have adopted the balanced scorecard approach (Creelman, 2001). The HR profession has not been as aggressive in implementing better measurement techniques. In 2001 an HR measurement survey was commissioned by the publishing firm Business Intelligence. Participants were senior HR leaders (Creelman, 2001). Just over one in three respondents indicated they were using a performance measurement (scorecard) framework. In turn, 86 percent of the respondents believed that the use of measurement would increase in HR over the next two years. During the last few years, business leaders have begun to ask HR to demonstrate the value it brings to the organization. HR is moving toward a more strategic role, and the use of HR balanced scorecards is increasing. That scorecard operationalizes the strategy of the HR function and includes financial, customer, internal, and learning and growth measures.

Developing measures of both HR efficiency and effectiveness for the balanced scorecard is critical. Efficiency measures relating to function cost are more solidly established HR measures and they are easier to track and report. HR effectiveness measures, such as measuring the impact of a recruiting initiative or the return-on-investment of a training course, are not as well established and are more difficult for HR departments to track and report. The conventional balanced scorecard often cascades from the corporate level through divisions, business units, and functions. It is important to note that HR can create a balanced scorecard even when an enterprise or corporate balanced scorecard does not exist (Creelman, 2001). This is possible when there are clear understandings of the corporate strategy and of the personnel capability requirements. Such understandings enable HR to be more proactive in creating balanced scorecards to measure and evaluate impact, and HR will need to take a more proactive role in measuring the effectiveness of their organizations so as to meet the requests of the business leaders.

## Training Scorecards

A training department might have some of the following objectives:

- to facilitate learning
- to enable behavior change
- to improve on-the-job performance
- to affect business results
- to increase employee satisfaction
- to improve employee retention
- to create a positive ROI for the company.

How is a training department going to know if it has accomplished its objectives? The training scorecard is a tool to ensure that the training organization is focused on accomplishing training objectives linked to business strategy. The scorecard provides a structure for establishing, tracking, compiling, analyzing, and communicating training results. It should be customized on the basis of business needs and may contain a variety of measures for what the business views as critical. A scorecard can be created and implemented even when there is no HR or corporate scorecard. This is critical because it enables the training department to take a proactive stance in creating measurement and evaluation strategies and to become a valued business partner.

As the studies conducted by ASTD, Jack Phillips, and Business Intelligence indicate, business is placing greater pressure on HR and on training and development to show a return-on-investment. Measurement and evaluation tools for training organizations, such as the training scorecard, are evolving because of a shift in accountability. Training organizations today must be accountable, justify expenditures, demonstrate performance improvement, deliver results-based training, improve processes, and be proactive. Using measurement and evaluation tools in training organizations can no longer be a reactive decision. The leaders of training organizations realize that business leaders are expecting to see results for the dollars invested in training, and proactively they are measuring the results of training initiatives.

The training scorecard enables executives to understand the benefits of the training program to employees and to the organization's bottom line. It also provides useful measures for the training and development staff, which can determine how well a program is working and improve or halt the program as necessary. A focus on using measurement and evaluation for the continuous improvement of training programs can build the credibility of the training department. The data from a training scorecard can be used to justify expenditures, build a business case for requesting additional budget dollars, and create management support.

## Creating Training Scorecards

When creating a training scorecard it is important to conduct a needs assessment and create a project plan to address the following questions: Why? Who? Where? When? What? and How? The answers to these questions will be important in deciding the scorecard's structure and components.

1. *Why is the training scorecard being created?* A training scorecard being created because there is a corporate or an HR scorecard should have direct linkages to those other scorecards. A training scorecard being created proactively with no other scorecards in place will need to have a linkage to the business strategy. Business strategy linkages can be made by reviewing a company's vision, mission, and goals for the year.

2. *Who is the target audience for the training scorecard?* The information that is tracked, collected, and compiled for the scorecard will vary, depending on who the target audience is or if there is more than one target audience. If the audience is the training department or a variety of company training organizations, the scorecard may contain data more relevant to continuous improvement training programs. If the target audience is senior executives, then business metrics such as ROI may be needed. Identify the target audience(s) for the training scorecard and perform a needs assessment to learn what measures are important to each audience.

3. *Where will the training scorecard be maintained?* The scorecard is often the compilation of data for multiple training departments. An owner should be assigned to the scorecard—someone who takes responsibility for creating the structure of the card and for ensuring that design input is received from all involved parties. Someone also needs to be accountable for collecting, compiling, and reporting the training scorecard data. Ensure that there are adequate numbers of trained employees to maintain the scorecard on an ongoing basis.

4. *When will training scorecard data be reported?* A reporting schedule is one component of the project plan for the scorecard. The data can be reported at a variety of times. The reporting could be program based, with the data calculated and reported on the bases of program completion and associated timeframes for behavior change and

business impact. Alternatively, the reporting could be calendar based, with the available data for all programs reported monthly or quarterly.

5. *What data will the training scorecard contain?* The answers to why? who? and when? will start to provide information concerning what data will be tracked, compiled, and reported on the training scorecard. It could contain data from a variety of training organizations within the same company, or from only one training organization. Participant satisfaction, learning, and behavior change data could be tracked, compiled, and reported for all programs or for only a designated percentage of programs. Data demonstrating the business impact of training programs might be collected and reported as cost-benefit ratios and ROI percentages.

6. *How will the data be tracked, collected, compiled, analyzed, and reported?* No two training scorecards will necessarily look identical, but they probably will use similar training measurement and evaluation methodologies. The scorecard measurement and evaluation methods are based on Donald L. Kirkpatrick's (1998) framework of four levels of evaluation and on the ROI process created by Jack J. Phillips (1997). The next section on training scorecard methodology provides an overview of Kirkpatrick's and Phillips's training measurement and evaluation strategies.

## Training Scorecard Methodology

When implementing a training scorecard it is important to track, collect, compile, analyze, and report six different types of training data collected over different time periods. These types of data are indicators, reaction, learning, application, business impact, and return-on-investment (Kirkpatrick, 1998; Phillips, 1997).

- *Indicators.* This is the traditional approach to reporting training data. Some examples of indicators are
  — number of employees trained
  — total training hours
  — training hours per employee
  — training investment as a percentage of payroll
  — cost per participant.
  Although these measures are necessary, they do not reflect the results of the training program. There are many types of indicators, but it is most important to include in the scorecard the measures of interest to the organization's top managers.
- *Level 1: Reaction.* This tends to be the most popular level of measurement in traditional training organizations, often used to measure 100 per-

cent of an organization's training programs. Reaction represents an important area of measurement, primarily for the training and development staff. At this level, participants' reactions to and satisfaction with the training program are measured. Sometimes the planned actions of the participants attending the training program are also captured, and that assists with forecasting program outcomes. Some recommended data to capture on Level 1 instruments are

— relevance of training to job
— recommendation of training to others
— importance of information received
— intention to use skills/knowledge acquired.

Those four items have predictive validity for projecting actual applications (Phillips and Phillips, in press) and should be compared from one program to another.

- *Level 2: Learning.* Learning measurements typically are not tracked for 100 percent of an organization's training programs. The percentage often ranges from 40 percent to 80 percent, depending on the definition of learning (Phillips and Phillips, in press). Learning can be measured informally with self-assessments, team assessments, or facilitator assessments; or formally with objective tests, performance testing, or simulations. Learning self-assessments may ask participants to rate the following items:

  — understanding of the skills/knowledge acquired
  — ability to use the skills/knowledge acquired
  — confidence in the use of skills/knowledge acquired.

- *Level 3: Application.* This level measures changes in on-the-job behavior while the training is applied or implemented. The percentage of training programs for which this measure is tracked typically is 20 percent to 50 percent (Phillips and Phillips, in press). This information often is collected through a follow-up survey or questionnaire. Key questions asked concern

  — the importance of the skills/knowledge back on the job
  — the frequency of use of the new skills/knowledge
  — the effectiveness of the skills/knowledge when applied on the job.

  Information also is collected about the barriers and enablers to application of the new skills/knowledge. Barrier information provides insight into the reasons for unsuccessful application of the new skills/knowledge. Enabler information provides insight into reasons for successful implementation of a training program.

- *Level 4: Business Impact.* At this level the actual business results of the training program are identified. The percentage of training

programs for which this measure is tracked is typically 10 percent to 20 percent (Phillips and Phillips, in press). A paper-based or automated follow-up questionnaire can be used to gather this data. Depending on the training programs' performance and business objectives, data may be gathered on the following:
— productivity
— quality
— cost control
— customer satisfaction.
There also are several other possible measures of business impact. It is important to include the method used to isolate the effects of the training program, such as control groups, trend line analysis, or participants' estimates.

- *Level 5: Return-on-Investment.* At this level the monetary benefits of the program are compared with the cost of the program. Approximately 5 percent to 10 percent of training programs are evaluated at this level (Phillips and Phillips, in press). The costs of the program must be fully loaded. The methods used to convert data should be reported. The ROI calculation for a training program is identical to the ROI ratio for any other business investment:

$$ROI\,(\%) = ([benefits - costs]/costs) \times 100$$

A benefit-cost ratio may also be calculated by dividing costs into benefits.

- *Intangible Benefits.* Intangible benefits are measures that are intentionally not converted to monetary values because the conversion to monetary data would be too subjective. It is important to capture and report intangible benefits of the training program, such as
— increased job satisfaction
— reduced conflicts
— reduced stress
— improved teamwork.
There are a variety of other intangible measures. These types of measures are often very important to the organization.

Figure 1 provides an example of one training scorecard template. The structure and contents of an organization's scorecard will depend on the needs assessment conducted and the answers to the questions who? what? when? where? why? and how? The scorecard example in figure 1 will be discussed further in the Nextel case that begins on page 41.

**Figure 1. Template for a training scorecard.**

| Training Scorecard | | | | |
|---|---|---|---|---|
| *Program Title:*<br>*Target Audience:* Indicators<br>*Duration:* Indicators<br>*Business Objectives:* | | | | |
| **Results** | | | | |
| **Satisfaction** | **Learning** | **Application** | **Tangible Benefits** | **Intangible Benefits** |
| Level 1 | Level 2 | Level 3 | Levels 4 and 5 | |
| *Technique to Isolate Effects of Program:*<br>*Technique to Convert Data to Monetary Value:*<br>*Fully Loaded Program Costs:*<br>*Barriers to Application of Skills:*<br>*Recommendations:* | | | | |

## Training Scorecard Challenges

There are several challenges an organization may face when implementing a training scorecard, and the challenges must be addressed during the initial planning process to ensure a successful implementation. Some challenges that may be encountered are the following:

- *Getting the buy-in of line management and the training and development staff.* As the training department moves from reporting the more traditional measures of number of attendees and number of training hours, line management and the training staff must be educated about the training scorecard process to ensure their buy-in. Line management may be concerned about the follow-up surveys and how the data will be used. The training staff may fear that data showing no behavior change or a negative ROI could imperil their jobs. It is critical to emphasize that the data is being collected to enhance training programs and improve business results.
- *Making the time to do the required needs assessment.* It is important that the training scorecard tracks the right information, for the right departments, and for the right reason (to improve business results). An effective needs assessment is required to align the training scorecard with business strategy and to ensure the gathering of appropriate

data. The needs assessment is also a way to ensure buy-in from executives, management, and the training staff. This assessment will take time.

- *Allocating the resources to create, maintain, and report results.* An organization that is dedicated to implementing a training scorecard will need to allocate the appropriate resources. These may be dedicated resources or the scorecard may become the part-time responsibility of several individuals. The scorecard initiative will not be successful without adequate resources assigned to the task.
- *Educating the training and development staff.* To implement the measurement and evaluation methodology required to collect the data for the training scorecard, the training and development staff will need to receive training. It will be important for everyone in the training organization to have a foundational understanding of training measurement and evaluation. Those people who are responsible for creating and maintaining the scorecard will need more in-depth training. For the scorecard initiative to be successful, it is critical to build internal measurement and evaluation capability.

## Training Scorecard Benefits

A scorecard can be implemented successfully in *any* organization. The benefits of implementing a training scorecard far outweigh the challenges. Here are a few of the benefits that training departments have realized:

- Management develops an understanding of the benefits of training programs.
- The training department is viewed as adding value to the bottom line.
- The training department becomes very focused on delivering only training programs directly linked to the business strategy, and this results in a positive return-on-investment.
- The training scorecard data enables the training department to improve programs continuously or to discontinue programs that aren't providing positive results.
- The training department is able to assess whether the training has prompted behavior change and application back on the job—a critical measure of success.
- Employees receive training that has impact. Employees are able to see the value in the training programs they attend, and their perception of the training organization is enhanced.
- The training department is able to justify its annual budget. Budget cuts are not as drastic as in the past because the department shows a return-on-investment.

- The training staff receives career-enriching development in the area of measurement and evaluation.
- Communication between the training department and executives becomes more frequent. The training department is able to talk with executives in business terms, such as return-on-investment and benefit-cost ratios.

## Conclusion

Studies conducted by ASTD, Jack Phillips, and Business Intelligence indicate a need for training organizations to focus on showing their value to the business. The training scorecard is a tool that can assist a training organization in doing just that—showing its value. The scorecard can establish, track, collect, compile, analyze, and communicate training results. Training organizations simply need to ask the questions who? what? when? where? why? and how? when creating the scorecard. The cases in this book demonstrate the value of training scorecards. Read them to determine which techniques will work best in your organization; then implement those techniques. The benefits of a training scorecard will far outweigh the challenges. Focusing on training scorecards will ensure that the training department is always winning the game. Make sure your company knows the training department's score!

## References

Creelman, James. (2001). *Creating the HR Scorecard: Best Practice Strategies for Performance Management.* London: Business Intelligence Ltd.

Kaplan, Robert S., and David P. Norton. (1996). *The Balanced Scorecard: Translating Strategy Into Action.* Boston: Harvard Business School Press.

Kirkpatrick, Donald L. (1998). *Evaluating Training Programs: The Four Levels.* 2nd ed. San Francisco: Berrett-Koehler.

Phillips, Jack J. (1997). *Handbook of Training Evaluation and Measurement Methods: Proven Models and Methods for Evaluating Any HRD Program.* 3rd ed. Boston: Butterworth-Heinemann.

Phillips, Jack J. (1999). *HRD Trends Worldwide: Shared Solutions to Compete in a Global Economy.* Boston: Butterworth-Heinemann.

Phillips, Jack, J., and Patricia P. Phillips. (In press). "The Corporate University Scorecard." In Lance A. Berger and Dorothy R. Berger, eds., *Talent Management Handbook: Creating Organizational Excellence by Identifying, Developing, and Positioning High-Potential Talent.* New York: McGraw-Hill.

Van Buren, Mark E., and William Erskine. (2002). *State of the Industry: ASTD's Annual Review of Trends in Employer-Provided Training in the United States.* Alexandria, VA: ASTD.

*Webster's Unabridged Dictionary.* (1998). New York: Random House.

# Confronting a Future Crisis

## Saint Elizabeth Health Care

Paul Hurly, Nancy Hawkes, and Kathy Craddock

*The community health-care industry is dealing with an acute, deepening short-age of nursing and other skilled personnel. Various North American firms faced with a similar strategic human resource shortage have adopted a more com-prehensive approach to attract and retain key personnel—Talent Management. Saint Elizabeth Health Care began to use the balanced scorecard in 1998 to frame its exponential business expansion. Exit interview data confirmed that management training was a key retention issue. Saint Elizabeth Health Care has created a "Strategy Map" and a learning and development balanced score-card to extend the linkage between its operational activity and one of the or-ganization's strategic goals—to become an "employer of choice."*

## Nursing Labor Force Crisis

A devastating shortage of nursing personnel is looming across North America. Researchers anticipate that this shortage could have a significant negative impact on the quality of family and social life, escalate health-care expenditures, magnify regional disparities, shorten life expectancies, and depress North America's long-cherished high standard of living. The severe lack of qualified nurs-ing practitioners could become *the* major domestic political issue dur-ing the next 15 years.

Examined from the perspective of Ontario, Canada's most populous and economically robust province, the dimensions of the ac-celerating nursing shortage are apparent. The government of Ontario in the early 1990s commissioned the Nursing Task Force to respond to

*This case was prepared to serve as a basis for discussion rather than to illustrate either effective or in-effective administrative and management practices.*

the pending nursing shortage and other nursing issues. The government recognized that having an adequate supply of nurses is fundamental to the health of Ontario citizens. Accepting the recommendations of the Nursing Task Force, the Ontario government pledged in 1998 to fund 12,000 new nursing positions in Ontario's hospitals by 2002. As a result of attrition, retirement, demographic trends affecting the supply of people under age 25, and the brain drain to the United States, 10,000 of these positions remained unfilled by the end of 2001.

The average age of an Ontario nurse is 46. Most baby-boomer-cohort nurses began leaving the profession years before their normal retirement age, the victims of burnout, job dissatisfaction, and the lay-offs and forced early retirements used to deal with government deficits in the 1990s. Among young people under age 25, nursing is seen as "women's work." Although this perception is gradually changing, the number of university-age women interested in the nursing profession is in decline. This is partly the beneficial result of the equality movement of the 1970s, which has opened formerly male-dominated professions to women and has broadened women's career aspirations. The Registered Nurses Association of Ontario has estimated that "between 60,000 and 90,000 new recruits must enter the nursing labor force in Ontario by the year 2011" (Registered Nurses Association, 2000, p. 9).

The dilemma for Saint Elizabeth Health Care caused by the present and growing nursing shortage is acute. Without a sufficient supply of qualified nursing, as well as other health care personnel, the business objectives and strategic goals of the organization may be compromised.

## Organization Profile

Saint Elizabeth Health Care is a Canadian private, not-for-profit business providing a wide range of services in the community health-care sector. The other sectors of the health-care industry are physicians (private and community/walk-in clinics), hospitals, and long-term health-care facilities such as nursing homes. It is a dynamic, innovative, multidisciplinary organization best characterized as a "rapid-growth business." From 1997 to 2001, revenue and staff expanded at an average rate of 20 percent per year.

Saint Elizabeth Health Care began operation in Toronto in 1908 with a staff of four nurses. Under its initial name of Saint Elizabeth Visiting Nurses' Association, it delivered mostly prenatal and pediatric care in clients' homes. The organization expanded its role and staff complement gradually during the years leading up to World War II and immediately thereafter. By 1992, it had grown to roughly 500 nursing personnel operating in metropolitan Toronto, and the Peel and York regions. The name was changed to Saint Elizabeth Health Care in 1995 to reflect the expanded range of services and products that the organization now offers.

In 1996, the Ontario government introduced a new competitive model for the delivery of community health-care service throughout the province under the aegis of the Ministry of Health and Long-Term Care. In this "managed competition" model, more than 20 organizations, from the Red Cross to the subsidiaries of foreign-owned health-care providers, submit bids in reply to requests for proposals. The selection of the winning bids and all contract management is overseen by a newly created government agency, the Community Care Access Centres.

Saint Elizabeth Health Care's board determined it wanted to diversify and compete in the new health-care marketplace. To accomplish this goal, CEO Shirlee Sharkey assembled a senior team with extensive business and health-care experience. Together, they transformed the organization's culture into one based on speed, growth, and constant change while maintaining the strong humanistic, professional, and caring values of its nursing origins.

Saint Elizabeth Health Care entered the 21st century with the strategic intent of becoming a "global life organization." Its more than 2,600 employees provide a wide range of nursing, specialty nursing, rehabilitation and supportive care programs, services, and products through 23 service delivery centers across the province.

In fiscal 2000-01, the organization provided 2.7 million visits to 150,000 clients and their families, an increase of 12.5 percent over the previous year. Revenues increased 13 percent to $80 million. Roughly 40 percent of the clients were seniors and shut-ins. The balance was children, families, and individuals who required a wide range of health-care services.

Demonstrating its commitment to innovation, Saint Elizabeth Health Care in 1998 became the first community health-care organization to be awarded accreditation by the Canadian Council on Health Services Accreditation (CCHSA). It was the first community health-care provider in Canada to offer chemotherapy and other intravenous therapies in the home. In partnership with the world-renowned Hospital for Sick Children in Toronto, Saint Elizabeth introduced the Electronic Child Health Network (eCHN). eCHN provides online health information for children, their families, and their health-care providers. The organization's Nurse Care Manager Model offers its visiting nursing staff the flexibility to achieve greater family–work life balance. The model uses self-directed group practices for client intake, assignment, and treatment continuity. Unlike conventional hospital and workplace environments, the Nurse Care Manager Model affords professional practitioners autonomy and task variety.

In 1999 Saint Elizabeth Health Care decided to draw on its considerable experience in community health care and its knowledge management culture to offer a wide range of professional consulting services within Canada and abroad. Recent projects have placed staff on assignment in the Nunuvut Territory and the Caribbean. Saint Elizabeth Health Care markets a range of administrative and software support products, each of them designed, developed, and used in-house. The @YourSide suite of Internet-based information solutions is a recent product to emerge from the organization's Idea Factory.

The navigation team, comprising CEO Sharkey and seven vice presidents, was challenged by the sheer scope and enormity of the task of transforming Saint Elizabeth Health Care into a global life organization. Sue Munro, vice president of health services, assumed responsibility for three complementary endeavors: guiding the day-to-day operational growth of the business, preparing the organization for its initial accreditation review, and developing a health-care quality monitoring and response system. To accomplish the third goal and to provide a linkage to the strategic plan, she introduced the balanced scorecard into the organization in 1998. Since then, Munro has been one of the champions of the organization's strategic balanced scorecard. Implementation was supported initially by an external consultant and then by the addition of health services analyst Anita Keyes.

Following the successful renewal of Saint Elizabeth Health Care's accreditation in May 2001, the navigation team revisited the strategic framework of the organization. In the process, they began to revamp the original scorecard drawing on lessons and techniques learned from the Massachusetts-based Balanced Scorecard Collaborative. Two principles struck a chord: the scorecard must fit the organization, and the scorecard's development can be depicted as iterative.

Throughout the navigation team's strategic deliberations in 2001-02, three key themes were repeated: staff recruitment, staff retention, and knowledge management. The symbiotic relationships were self-evident. Sustaining the core community health care services and expanding the new consulting and e-business division required the retention of top-flight talent.

Since 1992, the HR team at Saint Elizabeth Health Care has been evolving toward a role best described by David Weiss's (1999) three-level process hierarchy. The initial level in Weiss's pyramid depicts the basic services most managers would associate with an HR department: recruitment, compensation and benefits administration, and performance appraisal. The final level of Weiss's model, business transformation processes, encompasses such activities as aligning initiatives, cultivating a flexible culture, implementing change and transition, and determining the ROI of human capital. Weiss argued that HR departments must strive to attain this third level in order to add value to their organizations. He suggested that HR adds value well beyond its traditional functional roles by helping senior management anticipate issues and ensure that human capital is fully available and optimally used. In today's business climate, HR groups still working at the first level are early candidates to be outsourced. On her arrival, Sharkey formed a small team of senior managers to provide strategic advice and direction. Although HR was very much a senior team partner, the organization's rapid expansion in the mid- to late 1990s and limited resources made it difficult for HR to capitalize on all the opportunities. The addition of staff to HR since 1999 has made it possible to fully leverage Sharkey's vision of an HR function that adds strategic value at all levels.

HR expanded its role into Weiss's second tier of activities in the spring of 2000, initially by aligning itself with the needs of Service Delivery Centre (SDC) management. HR leader Paul Hurly introduced a results-oriented change process to address service delivery concerns identified by the SDC managers. Throughout 1999 and 2000, those managers had become locked in a desperate talent hunt in the face of what seemed insurmountable odds. Nursing and home care staff were jumping from employer to employer, often after only a few months' service. For SDCs near the United States border, the situation was made worse by the relative disparity between Canadian and U.S. dollars. U.S. hospitals were siphoning qualified nursing staff out of the Ontario labor pool. Ontario hospitals began luring scarce talent like physiotherapists with incentives such as signing bonuses, a tactic commonly thought reserved for dot.com twenty-somethings.

Turning to the successes of General Electric, Hurly dubbed the HR change process "Work Out." The HR team identified and prioritized more than 30 issues and opportunities to improve efficiency and effectiveness. Team members, often in partnership with some of their internal customers, learned problem-solving, measurement, and analytical methods while they tackled the priority issues.

After 18 months, the results were dramatic. In one example of cycle-time improvement, the issuing of employment agreements was reduced from four weeks to 48 hours. The need for managers to make a firm salary offer was critical to signing a candidate who usually had multiple offers in hand. The process of issuing the confirmation of starting compensation was reengineered from two weeks to eight hours. Managers report they now often receive the confirmations in one hour.

In addition to reducing cycle time to provide frontline managers with the needed information quickly, the HR team members tackled several quality issues. In one project, a cross-functional team facilitated by HR made a 90 percent reduction in payment errors. The improvement reduced rework and increased employee morale.

The HR team recognized that to measure the impact of their overall continuous improvement efforts, the work team would need baseline data. A customer service survey was used to gather responses for 63 performance standards organized among nine functional areas. The format of collecting data for two dimensions—the levels of importance as well as the performance for each standard—allows the results to be summarized and interpreted easily in a two-by-two matrix graph. This method of data presentation, first used in customer service survey work in the late 1980s, provides managers and their teams with a powerful way to make data-driven decisions quickly (Hurly, 1997).

HR team members studied the principles and methods of Six Sigma throughout 2001. Eventually this led to the development of their own modified eight-step Six Sigma process. The team also was aware of the value of the balanced scorecard as a tool for aligning efforts, measuring results, and refocusing improvement efforts. By the fall of 2001, team members had developed a draft HR "Strategy Map" (figure 1) and had identified potential indicators and measures.

The team also decided to participate in Canada's HR Benchmarking Network, coordinated by Colin Dawes, director of compensation and benefits at Extendicare (Canada) Inc. This best practices initiative allows participating Canadian organizations to compare their HR performance across more than 30 indicators, including training program performance. Participating organizations then use the results to contact like organizations that are willing to share the reasons for their success. This national collaborative is in its 10th year.

As HR interacted with SDC management to improve its processes, support the service delivery centers, and align itself with the organization's business objectives, several managers began to request new services. One such request was to provide training for supportive care supervisors.

**Figure 1. HR strategy map, 2002-04.**

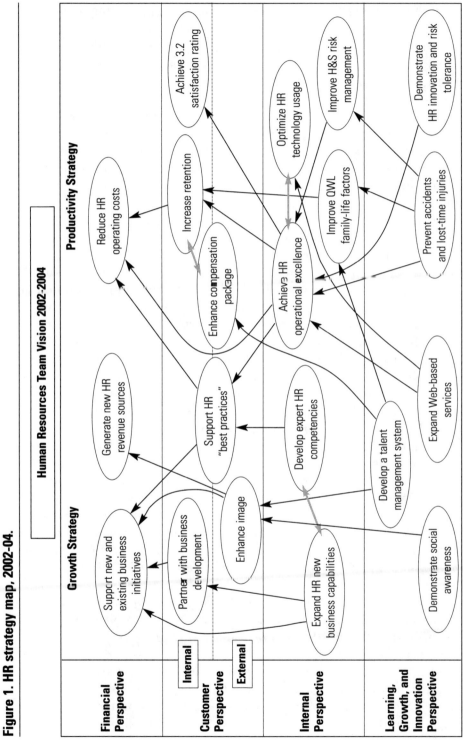

Human Resources Team Vision 2002-2004

QWL = quality of working life; H&S = health and safety.

## Starting the Management Learning and Development Program

Saint Elizabeth Health Care differentiates itself from many of its competitors by its commitment to knowledge management and training in clinical practices. All frontline employees are offered more than 20 in-house clinical skill certificate programs, such as one for palliative care.

Until 2000, Saint Elizabeth had never offered a comprehensive, continuous training program for its management team, although the concept had long had the support of the navigation team. Lean resources and insufficient numbers had not warranted the development of an in-house program. In October 2000, responding to a series of requests, vice president Hawkes, Hurly, and employment and learning specialist Kathy Craddock fashioned an outline for a supervisor training program. As they began to develop the outline, they recognized four conceptual possibilities.

First, all members of the management team could benefit from knowledge and skill enhancement while performing their daily responsibilities. Management team members were drawn from many organizations that generally had not invested in their growth and development. Second, the characteristics of Saint Elizabeth Health Care (that is, 23 geographically dispersed centers, a *virtual* organization, hectic schedules, variations in competence, and Internet-based services) and adult education (formal and nonformal traditions) supported the framing of the endeavor as "learning," not just training. A "learning" program would open the door to content delivery by self-paced, mentor-based, and other means. Third, management development could affect the extension and consolidation of Saint Elizabeth's culture significantly by aligning the human relations and performance management practices of new management with the organization's values and norms. Rapid expansion had diluted the cultural consistency and cohesiveness that had characterized the organization prior to 1997. Fourth, a management learning program could contribute to staff retention and recruitment—a hypothesis confirmed by management exit interview results in the spring and summer of 2001.

A cross-functional learning and development working group was established in the spring of 2001, with the assistance of Nancy Lefebre, vice president of knowledge management and practice, and Hawkes. This advisory body now guides the overall direction and support for the program. The management program's curriculum is based on a core competency model developed using Michael Zwell's (2000) model. Thirteen core competencies were identified for the management group, including accountability, creativity/innovation, leadership, quality and service, and business acumen. Each competency has a corresponding set of behavioral indicators. HR ensured that these competencies correlate with the responsibilities and qualifications of each management position as determined by the organization's job evaluation process. The result eventually will be a seamless, consistent process of employee job selection, probationary and annual appraisal, career development, learning program design and assessment, and succession planning based on an integrated progression of competencies from entry-level to more senior positions.

## Measuring Alignment

From the outset, Donald Kirkpatrick's (1998) well-known four-tier evaluation model formed the basis for assessing the impact of the learning and development program offerings. The development of the corporate and the HR balanced scorecards began to suggest that even a more comprehensive approach was needed. Clearly, Kirkpatrick's approach would help answer one key question often overlooked: Would management learning affect the business? The HR team wondered whether that was sufficient.

Was it sufficient, reflecting on the management exit interview data and other anecdotal information, to view management learning and development as a "growth factor," in Herzberg's (1968) term, that would increase retention? Or was there a need to look deeper for alignment and benefit from the learning and development program? Could the organization attract more and better managers by offering a comprehensive slate of learning activities? Would better managers strengthen and extend the culture, and thereby turn Saint Elizabeth Health Care into a magnet organization? If so, this would be a return to the enviable status the organization had enjoyed in the early 1990s as one of Canada's top workplaces for women (Frank, 1994).

Talent management has emerged recently as a strategy for retaining key employees and attracting others by transforming corporate culture. There are numerous books on the topic, but to date we prefer the description provided by Edward Gubman (1998). The health-care community has long described successful talent management employers as "magnet organizations" (Buchan 1999; Havens and Aiken, 1999; Advisory Committee on Health Human Resources, 2000). We are all familiar with those types of organizations. They consistently make someone's list of the top 10 employers. These employers seldom advertise or even use headhunters, except for the most senior vacancies. They are flooded with applications from people who want to work for them. The consensus opinion on the street among all of the occupational groups that these organizations must attract is that they are *the* preferred employer with whom to work.

Faced with the current and worsening shortage of nursing and health-care management staff in Ontario, and fluctuating supply and demand swings in information technology (IT) personnel, the HR team at Saint Elizabeth Health Care identified a talent management system as a tactic to address the navigation team's strategic human resource goals. The relationship between the impact of talent management and other HR initiatives will be easier to communicate thanks to the development of the HR strategy map.

Questions remain, however. Can a learning and development program play a role in implementing a talent management approach for recruiting nurses as well as managers? Could a balanced scorecard ensure that there were linkages with the organization's strategic goals, identify potential gaps, and pinpoint indicators to measure the contribution?

## Developing the Learning and Development Balanced Scorecard

The 12-member HR team primarily used the approach developed by Robert S. Kaplan and David Norton's (1996) Balanced Scorecard Collaborative of Lincoln, Massachusetts. The collaborative (www.bscol .com) is a professional services firm that facilitates the worldwide awareness, use, enhancement, and integrity of the balanced scorecard as a value-added management process. Some ideas were borrowed from the work of Becker, Huselid, and Ulrich (2001), but their seven-step implementation model violated the team members' stance on keeping it simple: "Although information is essentially infinite, demand for it is limited by the number of waking hours in a day. How you use people's time has become the key driver of how they'll focus their attention" (Jensen, 2000). The Collaborative recommends a three-step process:
1. Assess the strategic readiness of your human capital.
2. Build the HR organization strategy maps and balanced scorecards.
3. Implement the integrated HR strategic management process (Frango and Randall, 2001).

The steps the HR team used to develop the strategy map and scorecards are intertwined and so are described here as a seamless process. First, the HR team members reprioritized the performance issues not dealt with by "Work Out." Second, five priority items were selected for action in 2002-03. Third, the HR team reviewed the organization's May 2001 accreditation report of more than 10 HR and health and safety issues that could be improved upon. (For a sample of the report, see figure 2.)

**Figure 2. Sample priorities from the 2001 accreditation report sorted by the HR team.**

| Priority and Key Term Based on the Accreditation Standards | Related Accreditation Opportunities for Improvement | HR "Work Out" Priorities | HR Project Tracker "A" Priorities (3/28/02 Tracker) | Related HR Activities | Actual Completion Date |
|---|---|---|---|---|---|
| **2. Learning and development (education and training)** | **1.3**<br>• Continue to make revisions to the NCM model to assist the nurses to deal with workload issues.<br>• Continue to recognize leadership and train and orient additional resources to carry out the human resource plan.<br><br>**1.4**<br>• Continue to educate staff around the purpose and activities of staff association so they see it as a mechan sm to communicate with the executive team.<br>• Look for trends from occurrence reports for training opportunities.<br><br>**3.1**<br>• The evaluation of health and safety data is in process of being developed further.<br>• Further development of needs assessments for training opportunities.<br>• Continue to develop mechanisms to collect employee satisfaction feedback. | #2 Learning and development items 5, 17, and 22; Management training in policies and procedures, processes | 1. ESA 2000 changes<br>5. Revise content, etc., of orientation packages<br>11. Define management competencies; training framework<br>16. Design and develop supervisory training<br>15. Design and develop managerial training<br>19. Train staff association | Supervisory training started in November 2000<br><br>Learning and development working group formed to advise and oversee in spring 2001<br><br>Consideration of additional compensation for shift work<br><br>Compensation for specialty responsibilities<br><br>Development and delivery of WHMIS training program | |

NCM = Nurse Care Manager; ESA = Employment Standards Act, 2000; WHMIS = Workplace Hazardous Materials Information System

The fourth step in the HR process, consistent with the Collaborative's methodology, drew on the corporate map as a framework to develop the HR strategy map (see figure 1). The navigation team's revised strategy map cited HR readiness issues four times. The linkages showed the powerful relationships that already existed and could be enhanced among the various endeavors. The HR strategy map identified the potential productivity contribution that a talent management system could contribute. These four steps consumed about eight hours of meetings over a two-month period.

During that time, the team also finalized an HR vision statement for 2002-04 (figure 3). The framework incorporates design features developed by Gilmore and Associates, a training and consulting firm in Toronto. The Gilmore approach to developing vision statements and strategic plans (*Compete to Win Journal,* 1993) ensures that they are linked with annual operational plans—an intent consistent with the outcome of the balanced scorecard.

With the HR team's initial work more or less completed, learning specialist Craddock drafted a learning and development balanced scorecard. In addition to linking it closely with the HR strategy map and balanced scorecard, she included the work of the organization's recruitment and retention committee and the learning and development working group. The latter body is still finalizing its input to the various tools while rolling out the learning plan for fiscal 2002-03. Creating the first-draft scorecard occurred over a two-month period.

## Components of the Learning and Development Scorecard

Craddock and Hurly developed a human capital readiness report, according to the Collaborative's three-step process. That report pulled together information from the strategy map and the organization's HR accreditation priority report. Then they prepared a human capital development report that drew on the deliverables of the HR team and the learning and development working group. The result, shown in figure 4, allowed everyone involved to refine the indicators and measures and to ensure that there were no obvious gaps.

The result was a draft learning and development balanced scorecard (see figure 5). The card identified the linkages to be developed with the HR documents and activities, and gave the cross-functional learning and developing working group something tangible to critique and enhance.

The HR team then worked with Craddock to identify the linkages between the HR balanced scorecard and the learning and development balanced scorecard (figure 6). This check for linkages provided

# Figure 3. Saint Elizabeth Health Care HR team vision statement, 2002-04.*

**Champion an effective talent management system that enables the organization and its employees to meet their goals and objectives.**

| A Champion— which means | B Effective— which means | C Talent Management System— which means | D Meet— which means | E Goals— which mean | F Objectives— which mean |
|---|---|---|---|---|---|
| • encourage and promote<br>• nurture (develop and guide)<br>• work with others in partnership | • does the right thing<br>• produces required results<br>• values employees<br>• is measurable<br>• promotes pride in organization<br>• focuses on customer service that is:<br>  a. high quality<br>  b. related content feedback<br>  c. high customer satisfaction<br>  d. timely | • reward systems<br>• recruitment and retention of quality talent<br>• talent development<br>• career pathing<br>• succession planning<br>• performance management<br>• motivation and challenging of our talent<br>• alignment of skills sets with needs of organization | • harmonize with<br>• achieve or attain | • statements describing a desired outcome<br>• one to five year time from normal<br>• business<br>• organization<br>• work<br>• personal<br>• professional | • time-limited statements with measurable outcomes<br>• one year or less operational timeframe<br>• business<br>• organization<br>• work<br>• personal<br>• professional |

OBJECTIVES

*Based on the vision model developed by Gilmore and Associates (1992).

# Figure 4. Linkages between the strategic human capital readiness report and the human capital development report.

| Human Capital Readiness Report | | Human Capital Development Report | |
|---|---|---|---|
| **Human Capital Category/Objective** | **Measure of Strategic Readiness** | **High-Performance Corporate and HR Practice** | **Measure** |
| *Strategic competencies*<br>Identified, developed, and validated; plan developed to close identified gap. | • Performance management appraisals<br>• Self-assessment | • Talent management<br>• Alignment (competencies, appraisal, interview tools)<br>• Person-job fit | • Cost:hire<br>• Time:hire<br>• Employment activity report<br>• Assessments and appraisals |
| *Leadership*<br>Develop cadre of leaders at all levels and for succession planning. | • Employee satisfaction survey<br>• Performance management appraisal | • Leadership-management development<br>• Internal postings<br>• Staff secondments* to project | • Internal fill rate (percentage)<br>• Focus groups |
| *Culture*<br>Internalize shared values, principles, and norms. | • Culture survey<br>• Employee satisfaction survey | • Web-based orientation<br>• Staff association training<br>• Annual employee recognition<br>• The GLOBAL Award<br>• Saint Elizabeth Feast Day<br>• Newsletters—SDCs; employee; HR | • Culture survey<br>• Focus groups<br>• Site visits by navigation team and HR<br>• Grievance tracking |
| *Knowledge sharing and management*<br>Develop systems, procedures, and behavioral rewards. | • Catalogue of knowledge banked<br>• Number of people formally sharing | • Knowledge management program<br>• Group meeting guidelines and practices<br>• Preceptoring<br>• Clinical training program | • Focus groups<br>• Percentage of nurses with certification skills<br>• Evaluation of preceptorship |
| *Teamwork*<br>Group practices and other teams exhibit cohesiveness, mutual respect, and strong task orientation. | • Group practice attendance<br>• Productivity report<br>• Group Development assessment instrument | • Group values and norms<br>• Shared leadership and participation<br>• Facilitator training | • Meeting skills evaluation<br>• Performance management appraisals |

*A secondment is a temporary job transfer within a specific place of employment, usually lasting several months to a year. There is a guarantee to the employee that he or she may return to the original position when the secondment ends. An example would be an employee moving to a position at a more senior level or in another department made vacant by a pregnancy or parental leave. The secondment opportunity frequently is used for career development assessment.

# Figure 5. Learning and development draft balanced scorecard.

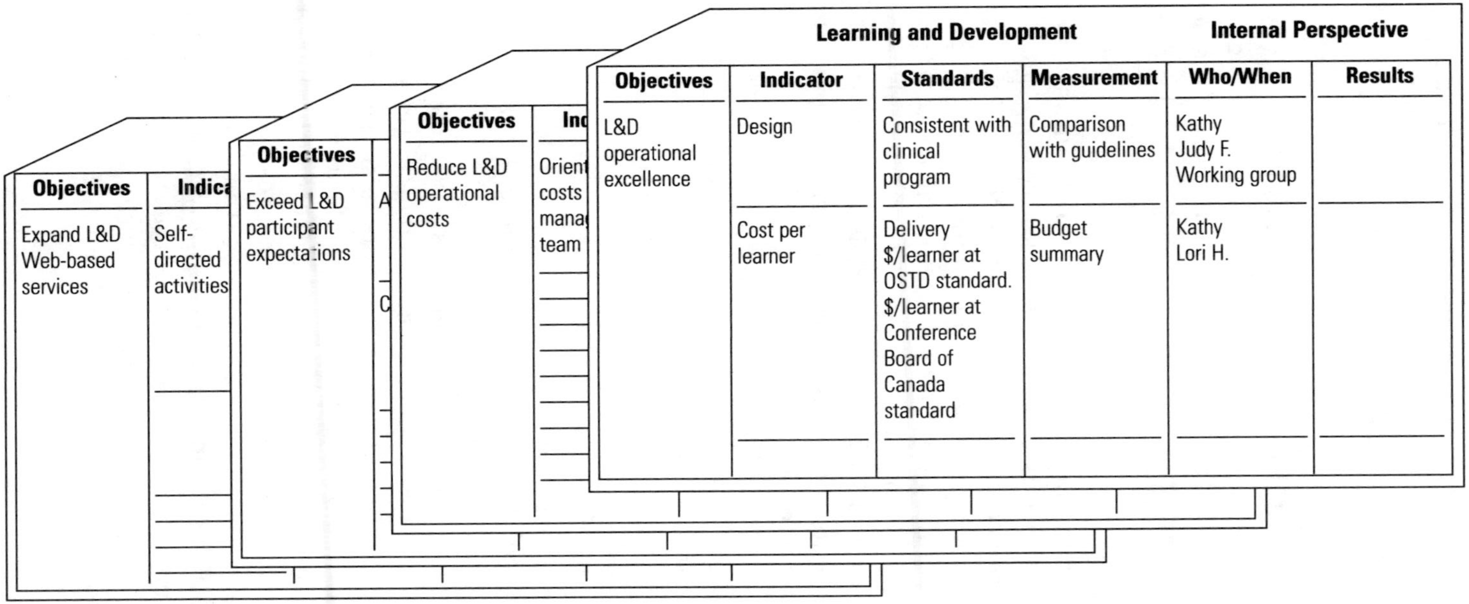

**Internal Perspective**

## Learning and Development

| Objectives | Indicator | Standards | Measurement | Who/When | Results |
|---|---|---|---|---|---|
| L&D operational excellence | Design | Consistent with clinical program | Comparison with guidelines | Kathy Judy F. Working group | |
| | Cost per learner | Delivery $/learner at OSTD standard. $/learner at Conference Board of Canada standard | Budget summary | Kathy Lori H. | |

| Objectives | Ind... |
|---|---|
| Reduce L&D operational costs | Orient... costs mana... team |

| Objectives |
|---|
| Exceed L&D participant expectations |

| Indica... |
|---|
| Self-directed activities |

| Objectives |
|---|
| Expand L&D Web-based services |

L&D = learning and development; OSTD = Ontario Society for Training and Development.

an important audit to coordinate resource allocation. In a fast-paced, interdependent organization like Saint Elizabeth Health Care, prioritizing resource allocation against multiple competing priorities is a challenge.

## Applying the Learning and Development Scorecard

The following review, employing two ongoing learning and development activities, will illustrate the application of the scorecard tools, indicators, and measures.

### Performance Management

The performance management learning program was started to address several needs. It was reasoned that addressing these needs initially would affect the customer perspective of the HR and corporate balanced scorecards, and ultimately the benefits would affect the financial perspective. If the literature on talent management and magnet organizations is correct, the ultimate benefit would be a more positive work environment and a greater emphasis on retraining and coaching employees with poor skills. That, in turn, would reduce the operating costs associated with recruitment.

This was not the case in 2000 when the organization's nursing turnover rate was extremely high. There were many contributing factors. One contributor was that some newer managers were handling poor performers in a manner inconsistent with the values and philosophy of Saint Elizabeth Health Care. There was a tendency to terminate poor performers quickly rather than to try to rehabilitate them. In the nursing labor market, with its acute supply shortage, the long-term effect of this labor practice might have been to deplete the labor pools of eligible candidates across the province.

What was needed, HR recommended, was a framework that recognized employees for doing their jobs correctly and recognized two key facts about poor performers: most poor performers will improve their behavior when their failure to meet expectations or follow procedures is pointed out, and poor performance can be handled as either intentional or unintentional (and progressive discipline is only appropriate for the former). Applying that distinction and other systematic methods builds stronger employee-management relationships. It also ensures that management action to the point of termination will be upheld under third-party scrutiny. We hoped that this fairness principle might strengthen the organization's appeal as an "employer of choice."

# Figure 6. Linking the learning and development and the HR scorecards.

| Scorecard Perspective | HR Scorecard — Sample Objective | | Learning and Development Scorecard — Sample Practice | Learning and Development Scorecard — Measurement |
|---|---|---|---|---|
| **Financial** | Recuce HR operating costs | | • Web-based orientation | Cost difference: staff involvement face-to-face vs. Web orientation [Level 4]* |
| **Customer** | **Internal** | Increase retention | • Management learning program | Management exit interviews; Management focus groups |
| | **External** | Enhance image | • Management learning program | Benchmark: hours of training/manager; CCAC site visits; Entrance interview ("magnet factors") [Level 3] |
| **Internal** | Expand HR new business capability | | • Request-for-proposal (RFP) writing course | CCAC RFP awards and debriefing sessions [Level 4] |
| **Learning, growth, and innovation** | Develop a talent management system | | • Develop career ladders | Number of employees promoted to leadership positions [Level 4]; Number of employees promoted to clinical consultant or resource positions [Level 4] |

CCAC = Community Care Access Centre. This organization arranges and authorizes payment for health care and personal support services for clients in their residences, whether a home or institution, and in public schools. Services are available to eligible residents of Ontario and are entirely funded by the Ontario Ministry of Health and Long-Term Care. CCACs purchase the services of Saint Elizabeth Health Care to provide health and supportive care services.

*The [Level ] references indicate measures deemed to address an evaluation level within the Kirkpatrick model.

Note: The figure demonstrates linkages identified to date. Further input from the learning and development working group will refine the model.

The performance management learning program is a three-part series of seminars for supervisors and a one-day comprehensive session for managers. There are also several refreshers, including a day-long simulation situated in a fictional service delivery center. The desired result, measured best by the employee and labor relations service provided by three HR team members, would include the following outcomes:

- Managers use the steps in the performance management system.
- Managers identify correctly whether an employee's behavior was in the intentional or unintentional category.
- Managers apply the correct form of response—either progressive discipline or progressive counseling.
- Managers write appropriate letters using the provided templates.

Additional talent management outcomes would include greater management retention, citing in part the learning program, and higher nursing retention.

Following Kirkpatrick (1998), learning session Level 1 evaluations have consistently demonstrated a high degree of satisfaction with the design and delivery of the program. The two simulations conducted in 2001 and 2002 have provided a Level 2 form of assessment. They generally have shown that most attending managers understand and can apply the performance management concepts and system when presented with case studies and problem-solving role plays.

Level 3 assessment is provided by the HR team members. Their observation is that roughly 33 percent of attendees can apply the performance management system to employees as taught. Roughly one-third of attendees have requested a refresher learning session. The last one-third generally manage employees as they did before taking training, based more on their past experiences and habits learned with previous employers. Performance appraisal with their senior managers may be required to direct these managers and supervisors to an alternate learning activity.

Level 4 assessment has not been completed. For the management group, this will require the introduction of a survey to capture information similar to the exit interview data gathered in 2001. Saint Elizabeth Health Care has not used a broad-based employee opinion survey, but it regularly uses focus groups and meetings with representatives via the staff association. Those two forums may be used in 2002-03 to gather data on the impact of several learning programs. Given the strong linkage to recruitment and retention and the cost of learning and development programs, the impact of learning and development as a talent management strategy is an important causal measure.

## Managing Injured Workers

In Canada, employers and employees are insured through quasi-government bodies for replacement income and other costs in the event of injury. Employers pay a fee based on a percentage of payroll. In turn, workers and their families surrender the right to sue for negligence. In Ontario, the insuring body is called the Workplace Safety and Insurance Board (WSIB).

The serious impact of workplace injuries is widely understood by most employers, so reducing and eliminating accidents is seen as beneficial. That is certainly the case at Saint Elizabeth Health Care. Employers who sustain a higher-than-average lost-time injuries record often attract notoriety as negligent and unsafe workplaces—clearly not the reputation on which to build magnet organization appeal.

Organizations may sustain higher costs than their competitors in the Ontario system without necessarily garnering public attention. A workplace injury experience system, dubbed NEER, tracks lost-time injuries per employer for a three-year period. When an employer's lost-time injury experience exceeds that of other employers in its rating group—for example, nursing care employers—the WSIB assesses a fine. The fines can be in the hundreds of thousands of dollars—sufficient incentive to motivate most sensible employers to emphasize injury reduction. In 2000, Saint Elizabeth Health Care received its first NEER fine. Addressing this issue would positively affect both the customer and the financial perspectives of the HR scorecard in much the same manner as did the performance management program.

There are two ways the organization knew it could return to a positive WSIB NEER balance. HR realized that eliminating lost-time injuries would be challenging. Given the virtual nature of Saint Elizabeth Health Care's labor force (most employees work in clients' homes and rarely visit their manager's office), efforts to reduce lost-time injuries would have to rely on professional care more than on supervision. Best intentions notwithstanding, injuries do occur.

The second best means of lowering accident costs would be to reduce the length of injury time away from work. Research at Dupont in the 1970s confirmed that workers who stay off the job longer as a result of injury become accustomed to staying at home. It is harder to get the longer-absent worker back to work, and the resulting insurance costs are considerably higher.

It was predicted by HR that improving the management of injured workers would positively affect the productivity outcomes identified on the HR strategy map (see figure 1). It was also, therefore, linked closely to the organization's productivity strategy map outcomes. Improving injured worker management would also affect in two ways the HR strategic "growth" goal to implement a talent management system.

First, by reducing the time that injured workers are on WSIB benefits and by facilitating their recovery, the organization's people-centered culture would be enhanced. Second, programs like managing injured workers are superior vehicles for helping management develop more effective behavior management and human relations skills. Soft skills training is notoriously hard to evaluate. Learners often report they feel they are floundering because they lack credible performance feedback. We have found that imparting effective people management skills in task situations, such as managing the injured worker, provides an empirical basis for learners and facilitators to assess the transfer and adoption of people management skills.

Credible evaluation feedback is important for two reasons. First, many of the skills needed to work with injured workers are applicable to the broader aspects of Saint Elizabeth's performance management program. Second, because employee satisfaction with the quality of supervision is a major predictor of retention, a learning design that would improve the development of people management skills would have broad benefit.

To start with, HR wrote new return-to-work policies and procedures during the fall of 2000 to guide how management would be expected to manage the injured worker. These were posted on the corporation's Internet-based policy manual in March 2001, accompanied by an overview seminar. The health and safety specialist then delivered a one-day learning activity to management staff at the organization's three learning centers. Evaluation followed.

Level 1 evaluations were positive. Level 2 assessment occurred during the two simulation learning and development activities and, for the most part, managers demonstrated they could follow the steps, maintain contact with the injured employee, and work with HR to return the worker to the pre-injury position in a timely manner. Level 3 results have not been as promising. Pre- and postlearning activity data show no reduction in the time taken off work by injured workers. When sorted by injury type, the results were more promising and significant (figure 7).

Back strain injuries have been the number-one compensable nursing injury in Ontario health care for years. This injury type is a major concern at Saint Elizabeth Health Care among both nursing and supportive care employees. The posttraining results for both the injured worker and for the organization were significant. For the

# Figure 7. Measuring the impact of learning and development on HR outcomes.

| 2001 | | Number of Injuries | Average Number of Lost Days | Average Number of Days Lapsed Until Modified Work Started | Average Number of Days to Pre-injury Recovery | Cost of Claims | Average Cost of Claim |
|---|---|---|---|---|---|---|---|
| Prior to October 23 | All injuries | 25 | 14.3 | 35.6 | 22.8 | $5,449.74 | $908.29 |
| | Back strain | 6 | 18.5 | 29.5 | 21.2 | | |
| After October 23 | All injuries | 24 | 20.9 | 42.4 | 23.7 | $2,117.87 | $434.37 |
| | Back strain | 5 | 9.0 | 17.0 | 12.4 | | |

Note: Some data presents partial impact measures for the Managing the Injured Worker program. Some of the data is hypothetical, for confidentiality

## Human Resources    Internal Perspective

| Objectives | Indicator | Standards | Measurement | Who/When | Results | |
|---|---|---|---|---|---|---|
| | | | | | 2001 | 2002 |
| Improve H&S risk management | Modified work and return-to-work programs | Days from injury to start of modified, average 15 Maximum of 12 weeks not exceeded | H&S statistics | HR; quarterly | 20.1 days | |
| | Claim costs | Average $2,500/claim | H&S statistics | HR; quarterly | $6,910/claim | |
| | Employee satisfaction | 3.5 on a five-point scale; SEHC is H&S conscious | Employee satisfaction survey | HR; quarterly | NA | |

H&S = health and safety; SEHC = Saint Elizabeth Health Care; NA = not available.
Note: Some of the data is hypothetical for confidentiality.

period examined, there were six back strain injuries incurring lost time prior to the management training, and five subsequent to it. Figure 7 shows that the total number of lost days for back strain injuries dropped by roughly 50 percent following the training. As a measure of management performance change, the number of days lapsed from injury date to start of modified work dropped from an average of 29.5 days before the training to 17 days afterward. The cost of the average back strain claim dropped $473.92, or 52 percent.

The data on the whole shows there is more opportunity for improvement in the management of lost-time injuries. When benchmarked with data from other industry rate groups for comparable lost-time injury rehabilitation, the Saint Elizabeth Health Care results are above the median. The data clearly shows management that follow-up is required or a further NEER fine may be incurred. A NEER fine or rebate, coupled with an assessment of external customer opinion about Saint Elizabeth Health Care as an employer, would provide two critical Level 4 evaluation measures.

## Communicating Results

Similar to management-by-objective communication tools, the balanced scorecard provides a concise method of presenting pertinent data. The learning and development balanced scorecard (figure 8) will be used to report program performance and its measurable impact to the learning and development working group, the HR team, and the senior management navigation team. Data will be compared quarter to quarter, year over year, similar to other reports from HR. The scorecard fits within an evolving set of organization activity and analytical reports that flow outward bimonthly, quarterly, and annually, depending on the time-sensitivity of their data, to service delivery centers. They also feed upward, where they are reviewed by the navigation team and discussed with the appropriate operating line management or support teams.

At this time, the work is still evolving. Reports are being coordinated and refined. We anticipate that duplication across some reporting will be reduced, thus saving time and avoiding confusion. More important, we anticipate that a greater expectation will be placed on proving that an investment in learning is producing specific, quantifiable, and desirable business results.

## Lessons Learned

We've learned a number of lessons:
- *Benchmark outside your industry.* HR looked both within and outside the community health-care and the broader health-care sectors for

**Figure 8. Reporting results via the scorecard.**

| | Learning and Development | | | Financial Perspective | | |
|---|---|---|---|---|---|---|
| | | | | | **Results** | |
| **Objectives** | **Indicator** | **Standards** | **Measurement** | **Who/When** | **2001** | **2002** |
| Reduce L&D operational costs | Orientation costs per nursing team member | $700 per employee (preceptor plus training) | Annual operating summary | Financial HR; year end | $825/ employee | |

L&D = learning and development.

Note: Some of the data is hypothetical for confidentiality.

innovative and best practice approaches. The finance, automotive, and steel industries are just three of the sources that contributed helpful approaches and program ideas, including the development of the balanced scorecard.

- *Be willing and prepared to adapt the work of others.* We had considerable debate on this point. Eventually, we felt it was inevitable. Strategy maps were conceived by Robert Kaplan and David Norton as a higher level corporate strategy tool. In HR, we adapted the strategy map to demonstrate the cause-and-effect linkages between disparate operational activities.
- *Facilitate broad participation in the planning and preparation.* Without broad participation by all stakeholders in developing the learning and development balanced scorecard, the resulting annual learning and development plan could well have been inconsistent. This required ensuring that all members of the learning and development working group and the HR team achieved a suitable understanding of the balanced scorecard and its related tools.
- *Communicate for understanding rather than insisting on consensus.* For large, dynamic, geographically dispersed organizations such as Saint Elizabeth Health Care, consensus about goals and strategy may never be attainable. The choice is whether to substitute command and control to force uniformity or to engage in a collaborative participatory process to achieve buy-in and understanding. The

latter takes longer. As a result, different people often are looking at slightly different iterations of the scorecard. But in the spirit of talent management, given that knowledge-based organizations naturally should be attracting bright, self-motivated employees, the bias has been to use a collaborative approach.

The need for speed also challenged the ability of the HR team to achieve broad understanding. The compromise was a process that would cascade back and forth among several groups and levels of the organization, while formation and implementation of the learning and development program was under way.

- *Communicate often and use as many channels as possible.* The maxim is true: You can never have enough communication. It assumes all forms. Informally talking up the value of talent management and linking the learning and development scorecard to the HR balanced scorecard interjected new ideas into conversations among managers and staff at several levels of the organization. Formally presenting evidence of impact to senior management built additional support to extend the learning and development program and to attempt new initiatives.

- *Refine measurement of leadership, facilitation, and interpersonal relationship skill building.* The HR strategy map depicted a more complex relationship of means to ends. More work is needed to develop and depict the relationship between learning interventions, such as the performance management seminars, and organizational elements, such as accountability and reinforcement.

- *Be open to the incremental development of the metrics.* We realized we needed to work harder to identify appropriate standards, indicators, and outcomes and to establish bona fide measures when designing and evaluating nonclinical training. Focusing on performance behaviors has helped. Some of the reference materials listed at the end of this case were useful here, as were the indicators and data provided by the Human Resources Benchmarking Network. Becker, Huselid, and Ulrich (2001) suggest that HR practitioners be prepared to develop, refine, or abandon measures as experience increases their understanding and insight.

- *Demonstrate the tangible benefits by implementing the HR and learning balanced scorecards.* A great deal of management-initiated organization change over the last four decades has amounted to smoke and mirrors, to sizzle without the steak. In the end, we were reminded of the salient observation of several consultants: The content of many organization's scorecards, much like their vision statements, begins to look similar. The real competitive advantage is determined by two factors that are organizationally unique. The first is the extent to which people within the organization feel ownership of and commitment to the written ideas. The second is execution. Planning without action was a pariah of the 1970s.

And, finally, the use of the scorecard measurement tool should predict and improve organization performance. Does achieving the results anticipated by the learning and development scorecard truly contribute to the prosperity and growth of the enterprise? Do the leaders of the organization report the results to the employees? Do the leaders use the data to reward and reinforce employee performance that meets or exceeds the standards? Do they galvanize teams into action and empower employees to fix problems and innovate when deficiencies, customer needs, opportunities, or environmental factors present themselves?

Those are the challenges still before us at Saint Elizabeth Health Care.

## Questions for Discussion

1. Saint Elizabeth Health Care made a whole-organization commitment to using the balanced scorecard. Can a training or learning program benefit from using the balanced scorecard without the commitment of senior management?

2. Saint Elizabeth Health Care developed its learning and development balanced scorecard at a point at which both the organization's and the HR's balanced scorecards were being refined or created. How can training managers, trainers, and organizational development facilitators influence the refinement and evolution of existing corporate balanced scorecards?

3. The strategy map is a tool to depict linkages graphically. What measures would you use to determine whether a cause-and-effect relationship occurs between linked items?

4. Is it possible, given multivariate factors, to measure the relationship between a learning and development program and an increase in employee retention?

5. Given that a learning and development balanced scorecard is at least two levels removed from the organizational balanced scorecard, what more should be done to ensure that the contribution of learning programs is understood by senior executives? By mid-level management?

## The Authors

Paul Hurly has more than 25 years' experience in management consulting, human resources, organizational development, and marketing communication. He has worked in the private sector and for both the federal and municipal levels of government. Hurly is presently the human resources leader at Saint Elizabeth Health Care. His private consulting has supported management in industries from financial and pharmaceutical to transportation and not-for-profit. He has coached more than 2,000 people to be more effective and confident in their roles. Hurly holds the Certified Human Resources Professional (CHRP) designation from the Human Resources Professional Association of Ontario, and the Certified Municipal Manager (CMM III) designation from the Ontario Municipal Management Institute. He was one of the first recipients of the Certified Training and Development Professional (CTDP) designation of the Ontario Society for Training and Development. He has a master of continuing education degree from the University of Saskatchewan. Readers can reach him at Saint Elizabeth Health Care, 90 Allstate Parkway, Markham, Ontario, L3R 6H3 or by email at phurly@saintelizabeth.com.

Nancy Hawkes has more than 20 years of experience in organization development and human resources consulting and management. For the past 10 years, Hawkes has served as a senior executive at Saint Elizabeth Health Care, responsible for the evolution of the HR, communications, and fundraising departments. Previously she provided organization development consulting services to hospitals, municipal and provincial governments, and organizations in the private and not-for-profit sectors. She holds a master of arts degree in applied behavioral science, a bachelor of arts degree in recreation administration, and a bachelor of physical education degree. Her continuing education includes completion of the executive program on negotiations at Harvard University.

Kathy Craddock is a registered nurse with 25 years of experience in pediatric, palliative care, and general nursing in both hospital and community health-care settings. She has managed community health-care programs that are responsible for supervising over 70 professional staff and 400 clients with Saint Elizabeth Health Care. Craddock is currently the employment and learning specialist at Saint Elizabeth Health Care. In this role, she coordinates and supports all recruitment activity across the province, and administers and facilitates the management learning program. She also coaches and supports the management team in resolving performance issues. She has instructed in palliative care nursing and supportive care training at Sheridan College and for the Ministry of Health. She has trained not-for-profit boards of directors in the volunteer leadership development program for Peel Region United Way. Craddock also was an advisory committee member of Ontario March of Dimes Peel-Halton for five years and a resource member of the Peel-Halton Palliative Care Advisory Committee.

## References

Advisory Committee on Health Human Resources. (2000). *The Nursing Strategy for Canada*. Ottawa: Health Canada.

Becker, Brian E., Mark A. Huselid, and Dave Ulrich. (2001). *The HR Balanced Scorecard*. Boston: Harvard Business School Press.

Buchan, James. (1999). "Still Attractive after All These Years? Magnet Hospitals in a Changing Health Care Environment." *Journal of Advanced Nursing* 30: 100-108.

*Compete to Win Journal*. (1993). Toronto: Gilmore and Associates.

Frango, Cassandra, and Russell Randall. (2001). "Measuring and Managing the Value of Human Capital." Teleconference presentation February 7. Lincoln, MA: Balance Scorecard Collaborative.

Frank, Tema. (1994). *Canada's Best Employers for Women: A Guide for Job Hunters, Employees and Employers*. Toronto: Frank Communications.

Gubman, Edward. (1998). *The Talent Solution: Aligning Strategy and People to Achieve Extraordinary Results*. New York: McGraw-Hill.

Havens, Donna Sullivan, and Linda H. Aiken. (1999). "Shaping Systems to Promote Desired Outcomes: The Magnet Hospital Model." *Journal of Nursing Administration*, 29(2):14-19.

Herzberg, F. "One More Time: How Do You Motivate Employees?" (1968). *Harvard Business Review* 46: 53-62.

Hurly, Paul. (1997). *Service-Quality Improvement Workbook for Teams*. Belleville/Oshawa, ON: Electrolab/HRI.

Jensen, Bill. (2000). *Simplicity: The New Competitive Advantage*. New York: Perseus Books.

Kaplan, Robert S., and David P. Norton. (1996). *The Balanced Scorecard: Translating Strategy into Action*. Boston: Harvard Business School Press.

Kirkpatrick, Donald L. (1998). *Evaluating Training Programs: The Four Levels*. 2nd ed. San Francisco: Berrett-Koehler.

Registered Nurses Association of Ontario and the Registered Practical Nurses of Ontario. (2000). *Ensuring the Care Will Be There: Report on Nursing Recruitment and Retention in Ontario*. Toronto.

Weiss, David S. (1999). *High-Impact HR: Transforming Human Resources for Competitive Advantage*. Toronto: John Wiley & Sons.

Zwell, Michael. (2000). *Creating a Culture of Competence*. New York: John Wiley & Sons.

## Further Resources

*Compete to Win Continuous Improvement System*. (1992). Toronto: Gilmore and Associates.

*Ensuring the Care Will Be There: Report on Nursing Recruitment and Retention in Ontario*. (March 2000). Ontario: Registered Nurses Association of Ontario.

# Using Training Scorecards to Prove That Training Pays

## Nextel Communications

Lynn Schmidt

*Business leaders expect to see results for the dollars invested in training. Human resource development (HRD) organizations have to be accountable, justify expenditures, demonstrate performance improvement, deliver results-based training, improve processes, and be proactive. This case study demonstrates how a training scorecard was used proactively at Nextel Communications to prove that training pays. The HRD organization implemented a training scorecard in 2001 as a tool to compile and communicate all of the data collected from impact studies conducted on core employee and management development training programs. The training scorecard ensured that the HRD organization was delivering training focused on business needs. The training scorecard also provided a way to easily communicate results to client groups, including executives.*

## Company Profile

Nextel Communications, a 2002 *Fortune* 300 company based in Reston, Virginia, is a leading provider of fully integrated, wireless communication services on a guaranteed, all-digital, wireless network. Nextel's four-in-one service—Nextel Digital Cellular, Nextel Direct Connect, Nextel Mobile Messaging, and Nextel Wireless Web—covers thousands of communities across the United States. As of August 1, 2002, Nextel and Nextel Partners, Inc., served 197 of the top 200 U.S. markets, and service was available in areas of the United States where

*This case was prepared to serve as a basis for discussion rather than to illustrate either effective or ineffective administrative and management practices.*

approximately 239 million people lived or worked. As of December 2001 the company relied on approximately 13,000 employees in the United States and generated annualized revenue of $7.01 billion.

## Training Organization Profile

In 2001 the training organization within Nextel consisted of approximately 200 employees who supported the development of employees in functional organizations, such as sales, IT, engineering, and customer care. Employee and management development were provided by the corporate HRD team, which conducted needs assessments and designed, developed, implemented, and evaluated HRD training initiatives. HRD field trainers were responsible for the delivery of employee and management training at a local level. The corporate HRD team initially implemented the training scorecard methodology in 2001 to prove the value of the solutions they were delivering and to determine how well training programs were working. This team comprised a director, two instructional designers, two training specialists, and a training coordinator. The training scorecard was introduced proactively by Nextel's training organization to position the HRD team as a valued business partner, rather than as a reaction to business leaders coming to the director of the HRD organization asking for proof of the value of the training solutions.

## Why Implement a Training Scorecard?

The director of the HRD organization realized that measurement and evaluation tools for HRD organizations, such as the training scorecard, were evolving as the result of a shift in accountability. HRD organizations had to be accountable, justify expenditures, demonstrate performance improvement, deliver results-based training, improve processes, and be proactive. Because of that new level of accountability, using measurement and evaluation tools in HRD organizations should not be a reactive decision. The leaders of HRD organizations were realizing that business leaders expected to see results for the dollars invested in training and proactively they were measuring the results of training initiatives. The director of Nextel's HRD organization believed that the training scorecard would enable executives to understand the bottom-line benefits of the training program. The scorecard also would provide useful measures for the HRD staff. They would know how well a training program was working and, based on the scorecard data, they could improve or, if necessary, stop the program.

## Training Scorecard Methodology

The HRD organization within Nextel used a training scorecard to demonstrate the return-on-investment (ROI) of several of its training and development programs. The scorecard used at Nextel (figure 1) contains six components, from training indicators, such as numbers of classes held, through the actual ROI calculation, and is based on the ROI process created by Jack J. Phillips (1997) and on Donald Kirkpatrick's (1998) framework of four levels of evaluation. The training scorecard is a tool that ensures the HRD organization is delivering training focused on business needs. It also provides an easy way to communicate training results to the client groups, including executives. The six scorecard components are described below.

### The Training Scorecard Components

1. *Indicators.* This is the traditional approach to reporting training data. Some examples of indicators are number of employees trained, total training hours, training hours per employee, training investment as a percent of payroll, and cost per participant. Although these measures are necessary, they do not reflect the *results* of the training program. There are many types of indicators, but it is most important

### Figure 1. Template for a training scorecard.

| Training Scorecard | | | | |
|---|---|---|---|---|
| Program Title:<br>Target Audience: Indicators<br>Duration: Indicators<br>Business Objectives: | | | | |
| Results | | | | |
| Satisfaction | Learning | Application | Tangible Benefits | Intangible Benefits |
| Level 1 | Level 2 | Level 3 | Levels 4 and 5 | |
| Technique to Isolate Effects of Program:<br>Technique to Convert Data to Monetary Value:<br>Fully Loaded Program Costs:<br>Barriers to Application of Skills:<br>Recommendations: | | | | |

to include in the scorecard the measures of interest to top managers. The HRD team at Nextel focused on number of programs held, employees trained, and total training hours.

2. *Satisfaction (reaction) (Level 1).* This tends to be the most popular level of measurement in traditional training organizations, often used to measure 100 percent of an organization's training programs. Reaction represents an important area measurement, primarily for the HRD staff. At this level, participants' reactions to and satisfaction with the training program are measured. Sometimes the planned actions of the participants attending the training program are also captured. Some recommended data to gather on Level 1 instruments are relevance to the job, recommendation to others, importance of the information, and intention to use skills/knowledge.

3. *Learning (Level 2).* Learning can be measured informally with self-assessments, team assessment, or facilitator assessments, formally with objective tests, performance testing, or simulations. The majority of the HRD training programs at Nextel incorporated a Level 2 learning self-assessment at the end of the class Level 1 instrument. Participants conducted self-assessments on any changes to knowledge, skills, behaviors, and their ability to implement the performance objectives for the training program back on the job.

4. *Application (Level 3).* This level measures changes in on-the-job behavior as the training is applied or implemented. This information often is collected through a follow-up survey or questionnaire. The HRD team implemented a Web-based process to collect Level 3 data. Key questions were asked about the importance of the skills/knowledge on the job, the frequency of use of the new skills/knowledge, and the effectiveness of the skills/knowledge as applied on the job. Information was also collected concerning the barriers to applying the new skills/knowledge. This provided the HRD team with insight into the reasons for unsuccessful application of the new skill/knowledge.

5. *Tangible Benefits (Levels 4 and 5).* At this level, the actual business results of the training program are identified. The HRD team used a Web-based follow-up questionnaire to gather this data. Depending on the training programs' performance and business objectives, data may be gathered on improvement in productivity, quality, cost control, customer satisfaction, employee satisfaction, and several other possible measures of business impact. It is important to include on the training scorecard the method used to isolate the effects of the training program, such as control groups, trend-line analysis, or participant's estimates. The HRD team frequently used participant, supervisor, and direct report estimates of the effect of the training program as

compared with other potential variables that might have produced behavior change. The tangible or monetary benefits of the program are compared with the costs of the program, which must be fully loaded. The Level 5 ROI calculation for a training program is identical to the ROI ratio for any other business investment:

$$ROI\ (\%) = ([\text{benefits} - \text{costs}]/\text{costs}) \times 100.$$

6. *Intangible Benefits.* In addition to tangible or monetary benefits, the majority of training programs will also derive intangible or non-monetary benefits. The intangible benefits of the training program may be increased job satisfaction, reduced conflicts, reduced stress, improved teamwork, and a variety of other measures. These intangible benefits may be extremely important to the organization and must be reported.

## The ROI Process

The ROI process is a comprehensive measurement and evaluation tool that provides results-based evaluation data and calculates actual ROI outcomes (figure 2).

In the Evaluation Planning phase, the objectives of the solution are developed and the organization is benchmarked against the objectives to ensure that the training to be evaluated is aligned with the business needs. The Data Collection phase includes collecting data during and after the implementation of the solution. Data is collected to assess the benefits of the course at various levels, including Level 1—reaction, satisfaction, and planned actions; Level 2—learning; Level 3—application and implementation; and Level 4—business impact. The Data

**Figure 2. Nextel's ROI process.**

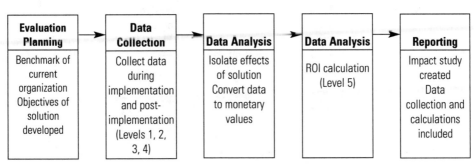

| Evaluation Planning | Data Collection | Data Analysis | Data Analysis | Reporting |
|---|---|---|---|---|
| Benchmark of current organization Objectives of solution developed | Collect data during implementation and post-implementation (Levels 1, 2, 3, 4) | Isolate effects of solution Convert data to monetary values | ROI calculation (Level 5) | Impact study created Data collection and calculations included |

Source: Based on Jack Phillips's ROI process.

Analysis phase isolates the effects of the training solution from other influences and factors in the environment. Data is converted to monetary values, the ROI is calculated, and intangible benefits are identified. The last phase of the process, the Reporting phase, includes generating the impact study to document the process and build credibility by showing the data collection and calculation methods.

## Training Scorecard Application

In September 1999 the HRD team, with the assistance of numerous HR teams throughout the company, facilitated focus groups with Nextel managers and supervisors. The purpose of each focus group was to identify the core roles and responsibilities of those people (figure 3 and table 1) and to identify topic areas for future training programs.

To address inferences established from the data collected from the focus groups, the HRD team developed several classes that make up the Nextel management essential curriculum. These classes included
- management law
- recruiting and hiring
- behavioral interviewing
- performance management
- managing corrective action
- an all-inclusive workplace (AIW).

**Figure 3. Nextel management roles.**

## Table 1. Nextel management role descriptions.

*Communicate*
Communicate clearly and concisely through multiple media across various organizational levels and settings. This includes communicating strategy, goals, objectives, performance, projects, and other corporate messages.

*Lead through change*
Help employees understand change and maintain results during times of ambiguity.

*Coordinate daily operations*
Exercise good decision making, planning, and problem solving to manage day-to-day tactical operations with your group and department.

*Guide performance*
Provide employees with ongoing feedback to improve performance.

*Develop long-term plans*
Create and implement strategic objectives for your department or group that support corporation-wide business initiatives.

*Motivate and retain*
Identify what motivates each employee and work to create an environment that retains employees.

*Build team unity*
Develop support across the team for organizational, departmental, and group objectives, while building a spirit of working together for common objectives.

*Coach and develop*
Aid employees in maximizing their skills and knowledge in their work.

*Recruit and hire*
Identify and hire the best people for the jobs in your group.

---

AIW outlined Nextel's definition of inclusiveness, why it is important to Nextel's business, and what managers need to do both personally and within their organization to enhance diversity and inclusiveness. Topics included diversity awareness; communication strategies; the influence of diversity in the workplace; and tools for successfully attracting, recruiting, retaining, developing, and managing a diverse workforce. The AIW course specifically addressed the following management roles: communication, motivation and retention, and building of team unity.

The HRD team, in conjunction with the field and operations groups throughout the company, rolled out the course to employees across the company. An ROI study was initiated for the course. All Nextel employees were required to take this course. There were two versions of the course, one for those with direct reports and one for those without direct reports. The impact study and training scorecard focuses on the version of the program for those *with* direct reports and typically is referred to as the "manager version" of the course. Through an online survey tool, more than 300 managers and more than 600 of their employees participated in the survey.

## Objectives of the AIW ROI Study

Nextel's HRD team conducted an ROI impact study of Nextel's AIW course for the following purposes:

1. *To measure the contribution of the AIW program:* The ROI determines if the benefits of the program, expressed in monetary values, have outweighed the costs. In addition, the study identifies the intangible benefits, those that cannot be expressed in monetary value, that are realized from the course. As a result, the ROI determines if the program made a contribution to the company and if it was a good investment.

2. *For continuous improvement:* The study provides a variety of valuable data for determining what, if any, changes should be made to enhance the program.

## Results of the AIW ROI Study

The data collection plan for the AIW impact study reflected five levels of evaluation (from Level 1—reaction to Level 5—ROI). The primary means of gathering ROI data was through postprogram data collection.

LEVEL 1 AND 2 RESULTS. At the end of each AIW class, participants received an evaluation instrument (figure 4) to determine their satisfaction (Level 1) and planned actions (Level 2). The evaluation included both open- and closed-ended questions pertaining to their *ability* to apply the skills, their *plans* to apply the skills, obstacles to implementing skills, an evaluation of the instructor, and a content evaluation.

Level 1 results were gathered from end-of-class evaluations for classes delivered between December 1, 2000, and June 30, 2001, at the company's headquarters in Reston, Virginia. Level 1 questions were presented with the following five-point scale: strongly agree (5), agree (4), partly agree/partly disagree (3), disagree (2), and strongly disagree (1). Those evaluations asked managers and supervisors to rate their level of agreement or disagreement with statements based on the five-point scale. Only items relating to the participant's reaction

# Figure 4. Level 1 and Level 2 evaluation instrument.

## Course Evaluation

*Please answer the following questions with your assessment of the training.*

Course Title: __An All-Inclusive Workplace__     Date:_____

Instructor Name: _____

| I now have the ability to apply each of the following skills back on the job: | Strongly Agree | Agree | Partly Agree/ Partly Disagree | Disagree | Strongly Disagree |
|---|---|---|---|---|---|
| 1. Identify and list the value of the differences that each individual brings to the workplace | 5 | 4 | 3 | 2 | 1 |
| 2. Recognize and address an inappropriate comment and/or behavior | 5 | 4 | 3 | 2 | 1 |
| 3. Teach my staff how to be more aware of differences to supplement companywide content in the program | 5 | 4 | 3 | 2 | 1 |
| 4. Explain my individual responsibility for supporting an all-inclusive workplace | 5 | 4 | 3 | 2 | 1 |
| 5. Design and implement initiatives that contribute to the Model for Success—An Employee Life Cycle (attracting, recruiting, retaining, developing and managing diversity in the workplace) | 5 | 4 | 3 | 2 | 1 |
| 6. React to and solve diversity-related issues in the workplace | 5 | 4 | 3 | 2 | 1 |

Identify one specific example of how you plan to use these skills on the job.



Identify one specific obstacle or challenge you will face when trying to follow through on your plan.



What can you do to overcome this challenge?

*(continued on next page)*

# Figure 4. Level 1 and Level 2 evaluation instrument (continued).

| | Strongly Agree | Agree | Partly Agree/ Partly Disagree | Disagree | Strongly Disagree |
|---|---|---|---|---|---|
| **Overall** | | | | | |
| I was satisfied with this course. | 5 | 4 | 3 | 2 | 1 |
| I would recommend this course to others who had similar training needs. | 5 | 4 | 3 | 2 | 1 |
| **Content and Materials** | | | | | |
| The course achieved the stated objectives. | 5 | 4 | 3 | 2 | 1 |
| The course content was well organized. | 5 | 4 | 3 | 2 | 1 |
| The balance between the amount of content and the length of the course was appropriate. | 5 | 4 | 3 | 2 | 1 |
| The course content was directly applicable to my job. | 5 | 4 | 3 | 2 | 1 |
| I have the necessary skills/knowledge to apply what I learned on the job. | 5 | 4 | 3 | 2 | 1 |
| I will be able to apply what I learned back on my job. | 5 | 4 | 3 | 2 | 1 |
| There was a linkage between the skills/knowledge taught and my needs. | 5 | 4 | 3 | 2 | 1 |
| I found value in the course materials. | 5 | 4 | 3 | 2 | 1 |
| **Environment** | | | | | |
| The classroom environment was conducive to learning. | 5 | 4 | 3 | 2 | 1 |
| The quality of the facility and equipment were appropriate. | 5 | 4 | 3 | 2 | 1 |
| **Instructor** | | | | | |
| The instructor's presentation was clear and understandable. | 5 | 4 | 3 | 2 | 1 |
| The instructor had an appropriate level of subject-matter knowledge. | 5 | 4 | 3 | 2 | 1 |
| The instructor answered questions to my satisfaction. | 5 | 4 | 3 | 2 | 1 |
| The examples, exercises, and activities helped me learn. | 5 | 4 | 3 | 2 | 1 |
| The instructor was well organized and prepared. | 5 | 4 | 3 | 2 | 1 |
| The instructor encouraged participation. | 5 | 4 | 3 | 2 | 1 |

*If you rated anything on this evaluation "Disagree" or "Strongly Disagree," please comment below:*

to the overall content of the course were selected for this ROI analysis because other items, such as individual instructor ratings, apply only to a specific class and not the course overall.

Managers and supervisors rated their level of agreement with the following statements. The number in parentheses reflects the average score of all participant ratings.

- I was satisfied with this course. (4.37)
- I would recommend this course to others who had similar training needs. (4.43)
- The course achieved the stated objectives. (4.45)
- The course content was directly applicable to my job. (4.43)
- I will be able to apply what I learned back on my job. (4.41)
- There was a linkage between the skills/knowledge taught and my needs. (4.26)

These findings suggest that overall reactions were very positive, with all average ratings falling between agree and strongly agree.

Learning (Level 2) was assessed in a variety of ways, including training activities, an end-of-class evaluation, and individual action plans. On the general assumption that a lower-level evaluation need not be rigorous when higher-level evaluation is planned, the majority of this level of evaluation was informal.

The end-of-class evaluation (see figure 4) included specific questions aimed at assessing participant learning. Those specific questions focused on the six objectives of the course, thereby reflecting key areas where behavior change could be applied or observed. Using the rating scale of strongly agree (5), agree (4), partly agree/partly disagree (3), disagree (2), and strongly disagree (1), managers and supervisors rated their level of agreement with the following statements. Average ratings are shown in parentheses following each factor.

- I now have the ability to apply each of the following skills back on the job:
  — Identify and list the value of the differences that each individual brings to the workplace. (4.34)
  — Recognize and address an inappropriate comment and/or behavior. (4.48)
  — Teach my staff how to be more aware of differences. (4.19)
  — Explain my individual responsibility for supporting an all-inclusive workplace. (4.39)
  — Design and implement initiatives that contribute to the Model for Success—an Employee Life Cycle (attracting, recruiting, retaining, developing and managing diversity in the workplace). (4.13)
  — React to and solve diversity-related issues in the workplace. (4.17)

Ratings once again fell between the agree and strongly agree rating levels for all six objectives, which suggested that managers and supervisors learned the skills that AIW was designed to teach.

In addition to providing learning information through an end-of-class evaluation, participants completed a personal action plan during the class (figure 5). Action plans developed during the program reflected those practices that participants intended to implement on the job subsequent to attending the class. The action plan form included information on tangible business impacts, action steps, consequences of taking those actions, and measures of change. Although this information was not gathered for the impact study, participants were asked to revisit their action plans when completing the ROI questionnaire. Action plans were linked to the specific business objectives identified for the AIW course.

LEVEL 3 AND LEVEL 4 RESULTS. Manager participants and their employees received an email with a link to a user-friendly online survey. The completed survey, which gathered information regarding whether these new skills were used, evaluated the impact of the class. The survey captured data that reflected Level 3 applications, business impact data (Level 4), and cost information and monetary information that contributed to Level 5 ROI analysis. The questionnaire covered the following topics: skill usage, ways to isolate the impact of the program, actions taken, results of actions taken, intangible benefits, barriers to implementing skills, and other benefits. It varied in format, with multiple-choice, checklists, time estimates, and open-ended questions. Last, the questionnaire was developed internally, was based on published ROI questionnaires, and was pilot-tested before use.

The survey link was sent via email to 592 managers and supervisors selected at random from the population who completed the training prior to June 30, 2001. The invitees represented a cross-section of business units and locations throughout the country and company. To boost response rates, HR organizations across the company assisted by having their executive line management send the invitation, thereby lending support and credence to the importance of completing the survey. Managers and supervisors invited to participate also were asked to forward an email to their employees with a link to a second online survey specifically for employees of managers who had completed the training.

As a further incentive to completion, ten $100 gift certificates were offered in a random drawing to people who completed the survey—five to participants on the manager and supervisor survey, five

**Figure 5. Course participant action plan.**

**Action Plan**

Name: _____

Program: _____An All-Inclusive Workplace (Management Essentials)___

Evaluation Period: _____

Follow-up Date: _____

| Tangible Business Impacts<br>The specific result targeted for improvement | Action Steps<br>What you are going to do differently to impact the business result? | Consequences<br>What will be different if you actually start taking the action? | Measures<br>How will you know if the consequences actually happened? |
|---|---|---|---|
| Improve Retention | | | |
| Increase Productivity | | | |

to employees of the managers and supervisors who completed the employee version of the survey.

In all, 320 managers and supervisors completed the survey, a 54 percent response rate. For the employee survey, more than 600 employees responded. The total possible employee target population is unknown, so no response rate can be calculated for that survey.

To provide verification and correlation of results, the survey for managers and supervisors and the survey for employees asked respondents to rate the extent to which managers and supervisors were applying specific skills taught in the AIW class. The questions were drafted as follows:

- *Managers and supervisors:* "The following is a list of behaviors and skills that were taught in the AIW class. Please indicate the extent to which you have increased the use of each of the following since attending the class."
- *Employees:* "At least three months ago, your manager took the class 'An All-Inclusive Workplace.' The following is a list of things you should be able to see your manager do after attending that class. Please indicate the extent to which you have seen him or her increase each of the following since attending the class."

In general, managers and employees reported similar increases in the managers' application of the skills taught in AIW on the job. The top skills for which managers reported some to significant change were

- exhibiting individual responsibility for supporting an all-inclusive workplace (86 percent)
- addressing inappropriate comments and behavior (81 percent)
- encouraging staff to be more aware of difference (78 percent).

Similarly, the top three skills for which employees reported their managers exhibited some to significant change were

- exhibiting individual responsibility for supporting an all-inclusive workplace (65 percent)
- identifying the value of the differences individuals bring to the workplace (63 percent)
- encouraging staff to be more aware of difference (60 percent).

In addition, many employees who saw no change noted that this was because there was no *need* to change in the first place because their managers and supervisors were practicing inclusive behavior prior to taking the course.

The survey also asked managers and supervisors to indicate specific actions they had taken as a result of this program: "Referring to your personal action plan and the main objectives of the program (increasing productivity and improving retention), think about one specific example of how you used on the job what you learned. What did you do? (That is, what action did you take?)" Some type of communication was the most often mentioned action taken. Managers and supervisors planned specific times in team meetings to discuss inclusion, increased one-on-one meetings, reviewed things from the class, and used the content of the program as a coaching tool for their staff. Many also said they simply started listening better and that enabled them to hear their employees instead of using their own assumptions and biases.

As a follow-up to the previous questions about what actions they took, managers and supervisors were asked to rate how successful they were in implementing those actions. Their responses are graphed in figure 6. The majority of managers responded that they were successful in implementing their action plans.

To measure business impact (Level 4) effectively, one of the critical criteria for selection of a program for business impact analysis

**Figure 6. Managers' and supervisors' self-assessed success in implementing action plans.**

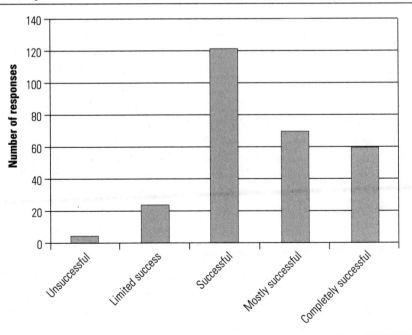

is the linkage between the program and the business goals of the organization. The selection of AIW for an ROI analysis was based on

- *company objectives*—the content of the program directly correlates to Nextel's 2001 People, Service, and Value goals
- *audience size*—all employees at every level are required to attend the program
- *visibility*—results are being monitored at all executive levels of the company.

Additional significant factors included management interest and the cultural impact of the course. The design of the AIW course also stressed how applying program skills could directly affect the business. Through the course objectives, participants were shown how productivity and retention could be enhanced.

Isolating the effects that the training solution (AIW) had on the business variable(s), in this case retention, meant identifying the portion of the results that was based on the training and the portion that was based on other environmental influences. Only the portion of the results based on the training was used in converting data to monetary value. This yielded a more accurate and credible ROI calculation. During the data collection phase, participants estimated the portion of the decrease of Nextel's attrition rate that could be attributed to the training and the portion attributable to other factors. According to managers, the portion of the reduction in turnover that could be attributed to the AIW class was 9.77 percent. This amounted to 36 people who remained with Nextel. This data then was converted to monetary value by multiplying 36 people times the $89,000 per-person cost of replacement value, totaling $3,204,000 in cost savings from avoided replacement costs.

The other part of the equation in the ROI analysis was the cost of the program, fully loaded to include all associated costs. The analysis of AIW for managers included all of the costs related to the program for those who attended the course from December 1, 2000, to June 30, 2001, as well as the overall amount of money Nextel invested in developing and implementing the course. Some examples of these costs are

- training costs for 1,254 managers who participated in the class through June 30, 2001
- co-facilitation fees for the vendor who helped to develop the program, incurred to certify Nextel employees to teach the course
- labor costs for the time that managers and their direct reports (320 and 600, respectively) took to respond to the survey

- all development costs for the program, even though the program was also delivered to all employees within the company and will continue to be delivered to new employees beyond June 30, 2001. The total cost incurred to achieve the benefits identified by the surveyed managers was $1,216,836.

LEVEL 5 RESULTS. The ROI calculation for a training program is identical to the ROI process for any other business entity: Costs are compared to financial benefits, and a ratio is determined. For this analysis, two separate calculations were made—the benefit/cost ratio (BCR), expressed as a ratio between the two, and the ROI percentage, which illustrates the net return per dollar invested. Calculations of ROI are based on 324 manager and supervisor responses to the survey. These responses are drawn from a sample of 592 managers and supervisors selected at random from a list of 1,254 managers and supervisors who completed the AIW program during the January to June 2001 timeframe.

Total benefits: $3,204,000
Total costs: $1,216,836

$$BCR = \frac{Benefits}{Costs} \quad \frac{\$3,204,000}{\$1,216,836} = 2.6$$

$$ROI = \frac{Benefits - Costs}{Costs} \quad \frac{\$3,204,000 - \$1,216,836}{\$1,216,836} = 163\%$$

Based on the BCR, Nextel received benefits equal to 2.6 times the costs of the program. Using the ROI percentage, the net return for every dollar invested is 163 percent of the value of that dollar; in other words, for every $1 invested, Nextel received a net benefit of $1.63.

INTANGIBLE RESULTS. Intangible benefits are so called because an estimation of the monetary value of these benefits is extremely difficult, and any monetary value assigned will likely be based on a large number of assumptions and estimations that would call that value into question. An example would be improved morale. Such a measure cannot be easily or convincingly stated on a monetary basis.

One intangible benefit was an increase in employee satisfaction as measured by Nextel's 2001 All-Employee Opinion Survey. The 2001 survey reflected a change in how employees felt about the value of diversity at Nextel. Employees responded to the 2001 statement, "Nextel does a good job of valuing diversity of cultural backgrounds, personal styles, and ideas among its employees." There was a 5 percent increase in favorable responses in 2001 compared with the 2000 survey. Unfavorable responses to this question decreased 3 percent in 2001 compared with the 2000 survey.

Respondents to both the manager and supervisor survey and the employee survey were asked to identify additional benefits they had derived from the class. A list of typical intangible benefits was provided on *both* employee and manager surveys. Respondents were asked to check all that they had experienced as a result of applying the skills of the class. The top intangible benefits for managers and employees are listed in table 2.

BARRIERS TO SUCCESSFUL APPLICATION ON THE JOB. Many barriers may influence the successful application of new skills on the job. Significant barriers may inhibit the implementation of new behaviors, even though a positive ROI is achieved. As a part of the AIW survey, managers and supervisors were asked if they have encountered any barriers that have prevented them from using, or *fully* using, the skills or knowledge learned in the program. A list of typical barriers was provided, and managers and supervisors were asked to select all that applied. In addition, an option of "other" was available.

The most significant barrier noted by managers and supervisors was time constraints. Sixty percent of respondents felt that time constraints have functioned as a barrier to using the skills and knowledge from the AIW program. Other significant barriers included finding activities that build cohesiveness and support other priorities.

Respondents provided recommendations for overcoming these barriers. The overriding themes of those suggestions included
- ideas, budget, and management support for team-building activities
- ongoing AIW training for new employees, and refresher training periodically for all employees
- more time to be proactive via additional headcount, filling open headcount, or lighter workload
- top management and senior leadership to set the tone
- reminders of key skills and knowledge via posters, retraining, email reminders, and so forth.

THE AIW TRAINING SCORECARD. The HRD team used a training scorecard (figure 7) to present and communicate all of the data collected from

**Table 2. Top intangible benefits for managers and employees.**

| Top Manager Intangible Benefits from AIW | Top Employee Intangible Benefits from AIW |
|---|---|
| Improved relationship with direct reports | Improved my relationship with my manager |
| Increased communication among staff | Increased communication among group members |
| Increased cooperation | Increased cooperation |
| Increased diversity | Increased teamwork in my group |

the AIW impact study. That enabled the HRD staff, program participants, and executives to see all of the relevant data in one place. The scorecard was a snapshot of training results. Data was compiled per program and, if required, could be rolled up into one overall report that reflected the training results of a number of programs. The scorecard ensured that the HRD organization was focused on delivering training centered on business needs. It also provided an easy way to communicate training results to the client groups, including executives.

## Conclusions and Recommendations

Based on the results of the impact study that was conducted, the HRD team concluded that the AIW program raised manager and supervisor awareness and helped initiate actions to promote inclusiveness. This contributed to reducing turnover, thereby saving Nextel the cost of replacing employees, and providing many intangible improvements in the culture and atmosphere at Nextel. Managers had the willingness, but they needed the time, resources, and suggestions to help them promote inclusiveness. The HRD team made the following recommendations for next steps:

1. Communicate the findings of this study to senior management and the board of directors. In the report, stress the importance of upper management support to improve inclusiveness.
2. Submit an article that summarizes the findings of this study to the company's electronic newsletter.
3. Add a regular column in the company's electronic newsletter that focuses on diversity initiatives within Nextel.
4. The HRD team should publish an article with additional team-building ideas.

# Figure 7. The AIW training scorecard.

Program Title: An All-Inclusive Workplace
Target Audience: Supervisors, managers, executives (1,254)
Duration: 1 day, 84 sessions
Business Objectives: Enhance employee satisfaction, improve retention, increase productivity

| | | Results | | |
|---|---|---|---|---|
| **Satisfaction** | **Learning** | **Application** | **Tangible Benefits** | **Intangible Benefits** |
| **End-of-class evaluation (1–5 scale)** | **Self-assessment on performance objectives (1–5 scale)** | **Manager behavior change survey (percentage increase = some change to very significant change)** | **Retention improvement results** | **Employee satisfaction survey: question #48—valuing diversity** |
| Overall rating: 4.37 | Identify value of differences: 4.34 | Identify value of differences: managers: 73% employees: 63% | $3,204,000 annually | 5% increase in 2001 favorable responses |
| Recommend: 4.43 | Address inappropriate comment: 4.48 | Address inappropriate comment: managers: 81% employees: 54% | **ROI = 163%** | 3% decrease in 2001 unfavorable responses |
| Achieved objective: 4.45 | Encourage staff: 4.19 | Encourage staff: managers: 78% employees: 60% | **BCR = 2.6:1** | **Additional intangible benefits:** |
| Applied to job: 4.43 | Exhibit individual responsibility: 4.39 | | | • improved relationships between manager and direct reports |
| Able to apply: 4.41 | | | | • increased communication among staff |

| Links to needs:<br>4.26 | Implement initiatives:<br>4.13 | Exhibit individual responsibility:<br>managers: 86%<br>employees: 65% | • increased cooperation |
| Action plans completed | React to and solve diversity issues:<br>4.17 | Implement initiatives:<br>managers: 67%<br>employees: 54% | • increased diversity |
| | Skill practice demonstration | Leverage team differences:<br>managers: 70%<br>employees: 57% | • increased teamwork |
| | | Improve communications:<br>managers: 76%<br>employees: 58% | |
| | | 79% reported success in implementing action plans | |

Technique to isolate effects of program: Participant estimates, estimating impact of other factors
Technique to convert data to monetary value: Standard values, internal experts, external experts
Fully loaded program costs: $1,216,836
Barriers to application of skills: Time constraints, finding activities that build cohesiveness and other priorities
Recommendations: Communicate findings, *Nexaminer* article, add diversity column to *Nexaminer*, provide additional team-building ideas to managers, continue AIW training for new employees, provide refresher training in 2002

BCR = benefit/cost ratio.

5. Continue AIW training companywide for new employees.
6. Provide refresher training companywide to current employees in 2002.

## Communicating Results

There are several reasons to make sure that the results of an impact study are communicated effectively. Communicating results can secure approval for the program, gain support for the program, build credibility for the HRD staff, enhance reinforcement of the program, enhance the results of future programs, show complete results of the program, stimulate interest in training programs, demonstrate accountability for expenditures, and market future training programs.

The HRD team created a complete report for the AIW impact study. The report was 61 pages in length and contained an executive summary, objectives of the study, background of the program, methodology for the impact study, costs, assumptions, results, barriers, conclusions and recommendations, and an appendix. A PowerPoint presentation was created that contained a summary of the results. The impact study results were also compiled into a training scorecard.

The HRD team completed its first and second recommendations for next steps, both of which were directly related to communicating the results. AIW impact study results were communicated to all of the participants of the study and posted on a Website where all employees could access the results. A presentation of the results was made to all of the leaders of the various training functions within the company, including the executive sponsor of the training organization. An article was submitted to the company's electronic newsletter, focusing on the results of the impact study and providing the link to the Website where the complete report was posted. The director of the HRD organization presented the results of the impact study to colleagues and peers at various conferences.

## Lessons Learned

A training scorecard can be a powerful tool for demonstrating and communicating the value of training to the organization. The HRD organization at Nextel learned several lessons as it used its scorecard:

- It is important to be proactive in introducing the scorecard to demonstrate the ROI of the HRD organization's activities. It demonstrates that HRD is a business partner that helps the business reach its strategic and operational objectives. Any training solution that doesn't do that should be identified and either improved or discontinued.

- A comprehensive training needs assessment should be conducted prior to implementing any training program. That way you are ensured that the training being evaluated is linked directly to business needs. Plan for evaluation early in the process.
- Select only the most appropriate programs to measure through Level 5. Focus on programs that are critical to the realization of strategic objectives, for example. This will ensure that the training scorecard does not become a costly and bureaucratic process.
- Educate others on the training scorecard components and share the evaluation responsibilities. Build internal HRD capability to conduct evaluation assessments.

## Questions for Discussion

1.  How can HRD become a valued business partner? What would your recommendations be to an HRD organization that needs to justify expenditures, demonstrate performance improvement, and deliver results-based training?
2.  Discuss the difficulties in evaluating the impact of a "soft-skills" management training program like AIW. How did the ROI process described in the case study help in overcoming those difficulties?
3.  Describe the needs assessment process used in the case study. What were the strengths of the process? What improvement suggestions do you have?
4.  Why is it so critical to isolate the effects of a training program? How was this accomplished in the case study?
5.  What are the advantages and disadvantages of using a training scorecard to compile and communicate training results? What data would you add to or remove from the training scorecard template?

## Special Acknowledgment

I would like to thank the members of the HRD team referenced in this case study: Ken Seemann, Christine Dellecave, Mike Feinson, Amy Kieffer, Susan Cardenas, and Cindy Setien. Their dedication to delivering a quality product and their willingness to put in extra time and effort made the AIW impact study possible.

## The Author

Lynn Schmidt is the director of the Leadership Institute at Nextel Communications. She has 17 years of experience as a human development and organization development professional in the fast-paced high-technology industry. In her current position, she is responsible for succession management, identification and development of high potentials, diversity and mentoring programs, and executive development.

Schmidt has extensive experience in the field of measurement and evaluation. She is certified in ROI evaluation and was president-elect for the ROI Network. She currently serves on the ASTD ROI Network Advisory Council. In 2002 she received the Jack and Patricia Phillips ROI Practitioner of the Year Award. Schmidt wrote a case study for ASTD's In Action series book *Measuring Learning and Performance* on evaluating soft-skills training. She has conducted several ROI/impact studies on such programs as change management, time management, performance management, and diversity awareness. She has presented at several International Quality and Productivity Center conferences and international ASTD conferences on the topic of measurement and evaluation. She teaches both needs assessment and measurement and evaluation at Georgetown University, Washington, D.C. She serves as co-director of programs for the Metro D.C. ASTD chapter and was a member of the 2001 and 2002 ASTD program committees for the annual ASTD international conference. Schmidt has a bachelor's degree in business administration, a master's degree in business administration, and is currently pursuing a doctorate in human and organization development. Schmidt can be reached at lynn.schmidt@nextel.com.

## References

Kirkpatrick, Donald L. (1998). *Evaluating Training Programs: The Four Levels.* 2nd ed. San Francisco: Berrett-Koehler.

Phillips, Jack J. (1997). *Handbook of Training Evaluation and Measurement Methods: Proven Models and Methods for Evaluating Any HRD Program.* 3rd ed. Boston: Butterworth-Heinemann.

## Further Resources

Phillips, Jack, J., and Patricia P. Phillips. (In press). "The Corporate University Scorecard." In Lance A. Berger and Dorothy R. Berger, eds., *Talent Management Handbook: Creating Organizational Excellence by Identifying, Developing, and Positioning High-Potential Talent.* New York: McGraw-Hill.

# Implementing Value Measurement: Return-on-Investment from Sprint University of Excellence

## Sprint

Joel S. Finlay

*This case study identifies the methods used by Sprint University of Excellence (UE) to identify, track, and communicate bottom-line dollar value measurement and return-on-investment information to its business unit customer/ partner. The Value Measurement of Human Performance Improvement initiative has developed over the past decade, much as Sprint's UE has evolved and matured. In its beginnings in the early 1990s, the UE was focused on foundational value in training and development, plus building credibility with customers and other stakeholders. The emphasis was on building working relationships, providing meaningful information on products and services consumed, and soliciting feedback so as to implement positive changes. In the mid- to late 1990s, the focus changed somewhat, with emphasis placed more on encouraging customer responsibility for learning, implementing continual process improvement, meeting or exceeding expectations, and driving operational efficiencies. In the 2001-03 timeframe, the UE has shifted to a more complex human performance improvement (HPI) emphasis focused on sustaining credibility with customers and other stakeholders, including increasing customer revenue production, decreasing customer operating expenses, and communicating the financial value of partnering for improved organizational performance.*

## Company Profile

Sprint is a global leader in the telecommunications industry, serving more than 26 million business, residential, and wireless customers in more than 70 countries. Sprint is widely recognized for developing,

*This case was prepared to serve as a basis for discussion rather than to illustrate either effective or ineffective administrative and management practices.*

engineering, and deploying state-of-the-art network technologies, including the United States' first nationwide all-digital, fiberoptic network. Sprint's high-capacity, high-speed network gives customers fast, dependable, and nonstop access to the vast majority of the world's Internet content. The company also operates a fully digital, nationwide PCS wireless network in the United States, serving most of the nation's metropolitan areas. It has over $26 billion in annual revenues and approximately 80,000 employees. Sprint is headquartered in Overland Park, Kansas, in the Kansas City metropolitan area, with more than 20,000 of its employees in the headquarters area.

## Training Facility Profile

The University of Excellence was created in 1990 to consolidate Sprint's multiple training and development functions. The intent was to improve the overall quality and reduce the cost of training. Sprint's business units were not required to use the UE's products and services, but the UE was expected to attract its customers by offering a lower cost structure than external competitors and by providing a better understanding of its business unit customers' needs and operations than external vendors could offer. It has met those challenges and grown rather dramatically to more than 600 employees, while delivering more than 400,000 training days annually in recent years. The UE's growth is depicted in figure 1, which identifies the UE's evolution. From a primarily training and development function creating foundational value, the UE has matured into a human performance improvement partner with Sprint's business units in creating financial value.

## The UE Connects Directly to Sprint Strategy

It is highly significant that the UE is aligned strategically with the overall Sprint enterprise, and that each of the UE's employees can track his or her contributions to the Sprint strategy. There are many elements that have worked to create this alignment, but the UE focus on bottom-line dollar results and ROI is a natural result of an intensive effort to establish and maintain what is referred to within the enterprise as a "One Sprint" focus. Certainly a significant part of this alignment is the cascading of the Sprint vision and goals to the human resources function, and within HR to the University of Excellence. Figure 2 graphically presents that cascade.

Beyond the organizational alignment suggested in figure 2, individual employees complete annual plans with quarterly updates and reviews through the LINK performance management system. For most

# Figure 1. UE evolution from foundational to financial value.

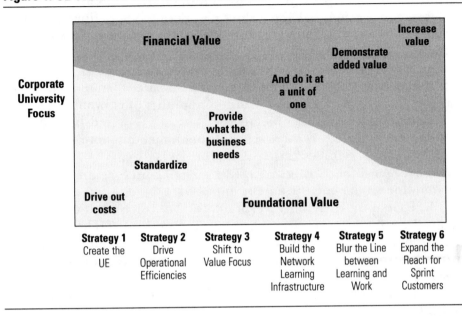

| Strategy 1 | Strategy 2 | Strategy 3 | Strategy 4 | Strategy 5 | Strategy 6 |
|---|---|---|---|---|---|
| Create the UE | Drive Operational Efficiencies | Shift to Value Focus | Build the Network Learning Infrastructure | Blur the Line between Learning and Work | Expand the Reach for Sprint Customers |

# Figure 2. Vision, mission, and goals cascade from corporate level to training and development level.

| Sprint | To be a world-class telecommunications company, the standard by which others are measured.<br><br>*Exceptional customer satisfaction—Inspired, innovative, and empowered employees—Superior financial results* |
|---|---|
| HR | To ensure Sprint's competitive advantage through inspired, innovative, and empowered employees.<br><br>*Workforce planning—Culture—Speed and flexibility* |
| UE | We provide Sprint employees superior development opportunities to meet Sprint's current and future objectives.<br><br>*One spirit—Superior team—Strategic partnerships—Customer focus—Best-in-class products, services, and performance support* |

employees in management or more senior individual contributor positions—approximately half the technical workforce—Sprint's Management Incentive Program (MIP) provides for literally line-of-sight objectives. Attaining those objectives affects annual bonus potential that might reach 12 percent to 15 percent of base pay in a financially successful year. Sales and marketing employees participate in similar incentive systems, but at risk for them are larger amounts of compensation tied to attaining sales volume objectives.

The UE's strategy is carried out through meeting key performance indicators (KPIs). In 2002, there are four KPIs driving UE overall performance. As shown in figure 3, KPI goals 1 and 2 relate directly to bottom-line dollar measurement and ROI.

KPI Goal 1: Hear and Respond to the Voice of the Customer drives the UE focus on bottom-line results and ROI. The customer relations management team (CRMT, usually pronounced "kermit") has primary responsibility for liaison with customer executives and managers. I provide primary support to CRMT members so they can be successful. Members of the UE decision support team do a lot of the behind-the-scenes work, providing for the interaction and involvement of customer business unit decision support people and supplying all of the financial and other value measurement reporting, both internally to the UE and externally to the business units.

KPI Goal 2: Blur the Line between Learning and Work also comes from the need to report the positive results of UE work to the Sprint enterprise. This is a challenge. As corporate universities like the UE use more efficient methods for learning, such as self-paced courses, computer-based training (CBT), and other e-learning alternatives to instructor-led training, the resulting reports appear to show that business unit customers are getting less for more—an outcome that surely does not look good to our customers.

Any training organization that has been reporting number of training days or hours along with costs is probably experiencing this problem to some degree. More efficient training methods use fewer hours, so the amount of training appears to be going down. Customer business units, however, are spending their full budgets—or more—for fewer hours of training. On the surface, the cost-benefit equation appears to be out of balance. Unable to find verified solutions to this reporting problem, Sprint's UE is experimenting with its own solution, using standard training equivalent (STE) units to represent all UE services and thereby to demonstrate that customers actually are getting more for their money. The STE concept simply works like "FTE" does in describing full-time equivalent employees.

**Figure 3. Sprint's key performance indicators, as they appear online.**

### Goal 1: Hear and Respond to the Voice of the Customer
Understand Customer Needs and Proactively Develop Cost Effective HPI Solutions to Meet Those Needs

| Key Performance Indicator | 2002 YTD | 2002 Obj. | 2004 Obj. |
|---|---|---|---|
| Successfully launch three initiatives per CRMT Account Team, approved by UE AVP, that demonstrate bottom-line (increase revenue; decrease cost) return-on-investment of at least 300%. (Objective for CRMT associates - see details for payout) | | ROI equal to or greater than 300% | |

### Goal 2: Blur the Line Between Learning and Work
Transform Sprint's Learning Culture Through Business-Driven Learning Technologies and Processes

| Key Performance Indicator | 2002 YTD | 2002 Obj. | 2004 Obj. |
|---|---|---|---|
| Increase in self-service | Begin measuring in September, 2002 | Registration Phone - 55% myUE - 45% | Registration Phone - 10% myUE - 90% |
| Standard Training Equivalent (STE) vs Actual<br>- UELive solutions<br>- Self-paced including CBT, CD-ROM, workbook, e-learning, etc.<br>- Coaching, consulting<br>- UEguide, OASIS, or hard copy job aid introduction or revision<br>- UEguide, OASIS or hard copy job aid usage<br>- Blended solutions | Being benchmarked in 2002 | | |

*(continued on next page)*

**Figure 3. Sprint's key performance indicators, as they appear online (continued).**

### Goal 3: Implement and Deliver the Right HR Technology
Identify and Deliver Business-Driven HR Technology Solutions with High Value

| Key Performance Indicator | 2002 YTD | 2002 Obj. | 2004 Obj. |
|---|---|---|---|
| Successfully complete the Sprint enterprise launch of myUE on or before 9/2/2002.<br>(MIP objective - see details for payout) | On schedule | Launch by 9/9/02 | |
| Convert at least 147 existing, UE VP approved, classroom courses to network-enabled solutions by 12/31/2002. Within 30 days of each conversion, classroom delivery of that course will end.<br>(MIP objective - see details for payout) | 10 courses converted as of 6/28/02 | 147 courses by 12/31/02 | |
| At least 70% of all courses activated (excluding TC50 and IS10) in 2002 will be asynchronous, via UELive or facilitated self-paced.<br>(MIP objective - see details for payout) | 67% as of 5/31/02 | 70% by 12/31/02 | 90% by 12/31/04 |

### Goal 4: Attract, Develop and Retain an Exceptional UE Workforce
Continually Develop the Workforce to Meet Sprint's Business Needs

| Key Performance Indicator | 2001 | 2002 YTD |
|---|---|---|
| Denison: Involvement, Consistency, Adaptability, Mission | N/A | See Goal 4 details |
| Employee Attitude Survey | 75 | Equal to or better than 75 |
| Forum on Workforce Engagement "Offer Fit" Index (OFI) | Benchmark through this year's research | |

N/A = not applicable.
Note: UELive is Sprint's name for its virtual classroom technology. OASIS is a proprietary complex problem-solving technology. MyUE is Sprint's overall operating system from beginning to end (from a Sprint employee-customer's initial online catalog/telephone inquiry to a record of the completed UE human performance improvement solutions for that employee-customer).

## Training Reporting Methodology

Since its inception in the 1990-91 timeframe, Sprint's UE has conducted Level 1 evaluations regularly, and Level 2 demonstrations and tests as required. Michael Homola, a sociologist with a strong background in statistics, took an enormous pile of Level 1 evaluation sheets and created a more nearly complete UE measurement function in 1996.

### Measurement Model

Homola began speaking in terms of Kirkpatrick's four levels of evaluation (1994) and of broadening the scope of measurement. Since 1997, under Homola's leadership, the UE has begun following the Chain of Impact, the taxonomy of learning measures described by Jack Phillips (1997, p. 43). (We should note here the historical connections regarding training levels. Phillips adapted those measures from the seminal work of Donald Kirkpatrick in the 1950s, which Kirkpatrick originally published in a series of articles in the ASTD journal, *Training and Development* [1959], and which he restated numerous times including in 1994 [p. 21]. Phillips's Chain of Impact measures range from Level 1, asking participants about their satisfaction with a development experience, to Level 5, calculating ROI for the bottom-line results of a development experience.) The UE has found it useful to use Phillips's Chain of Impact to plan and carry out measures of positive effect with Sprint's business units. Each of the five Phillips levels is described in the tables that follow. Table 1 reviews Levels 1 through 3, nonfinancial measurements of the value of development initiatives.

Level 1 measures are a standard part of the *UE Pulse,* an evergreen—or continuously upgraded—report maintained on the Sprint intranet by the UE data reporting project manager, who collects, analyzes, interprets, and communicates a large portion of the nonfinancial data amassed by the UE. The *UE Pulse* is available to all UE employees at all times. Customers may access this data by special request or through any UE employee. Sprint's Level 1 report is based on a seven point scale, and—unlike in 1996—is administered electronically through emails sent to participants following course completions. The emails ask participants to link to a Web address connecting them to the appropriate survey instrument. The return rate currently varies from 50 to 60 percent, according to Homola. He views that as acceptably high. Figure 4, presents this Level 1 data graphically in a copy of the online format.

The UE conducts a number of Level 2 measures but does not consolidate this data in any single place for reasons of confidentiality.

## Table 1. Perceptual and behavioral learning measures.

| Type of Measure | How Measured | Results Assumptions |
|---|---|---|
| **Participant satisfaction** *(Level 1)* | Level 1 measurement identifies the extent to which participants are satisfied with a defined development experience, usually in the form of a survey administered after the event has been completed. | This measure is based on the assumption that participants are able to recognize value for their time and effort, and that the UE needs to perform well in this measure to keep Sprint employees interested in using UE services. |
| **Amount of learning** *(Level 2)* | Level 2 measurement usually is accomplished by administering a test or participant demonstration of learning (i.e., skill check). | If a participant is able to remember knowledge gained or show ability to perform a skill, then he or she is presumed to have learned effectively from the UE experience. |
| **Application on the job** *(Level 3)* | Level 3 measurement is accomplished by observing participants at work (or simply asking them or their supervisors) to identify the extent to which they are using the learned behaviors on the job. | This measure is based on the assumption that if people are applying skills and knowledge gleaned from the UE experience to the job, work processes are likely to be improved, thus leading to the realization of desirable business consequences and improved business unit performance. |

## Figure 4. Level 1 evaluations (seven-point scale.)*

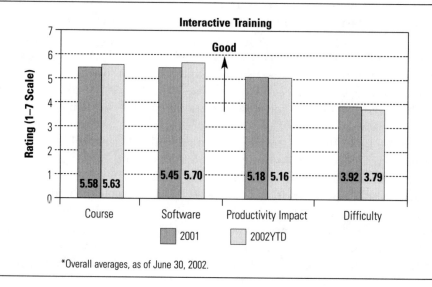

*Overall averages, as of June 30, 2002.

In regulated parts of the Sprint business, primarily in the local telephone division (LTD), testing and demonstrations are sometimes required, particularly of installation and repair technicians, although such requirements are much less prevalent than they were just a few years ago. In other cases, executives have requested Level 2 measures simply to ensure competence. Additionally, most CBT programs contain pretests and posttests, and many contain ongoing quizzes to provide self-guidance and to allow entry into more advanced parts of the courses.

Level 3 evaluation is more of a mixed bag. Level 3 data is not collected in a single place either, but evaluations are done as a part of many initiatives. In some cases, the developers want to know the extent of use of their programs. In other cases, assurance of actual use is desired to back up Levels 4 and 5 assertions of bottom-line results and ROI. In still other instances, Level 3 data is requested by a customer as a substitute for Level 4 or Level 5 data. This occurs in cases in which Level 3 data readily tracks directly to the bottom line. Such Level 3 data usually takes the form of a special report to a customer executive or as a paragraph or two in developers' notes.

In 2001, Carol Colston and I joined Homola in the UE measurement function. Colston helped build and continues to manage the automated Level 1 system, and I was asked to create and implement an integrated and comprehensive dollar-value measurement process for the UE. Table 2 describes Levels 4 and 5 bottom-line results financial measurements of the value of UE initiatives. Financial measures are particularly important to the UE and to Sprint because financial data is the common language of Sprint executives. In the past, many HRD functions, including Sprint's UE, have expected line executives to pay attention to HRD language for conveying positive news, and the UE only used financial language to report costs, which tend to be the negative part of HRD news. We reasoned, therefore, that reporting positive learning and development results in financial language seemed only logical if those of us in HRD wish to be taken seriously by line executives and seen as something other than a cost to be avoided.

## Scorecards Are Different in Sprint's UE

This casebook is based on the idea of using scorecards to report information to customers, but Sprint's University of Excellence actually uses scorecards in an opposite way. At Sprint, scorecards typically are documents that customers fill out, expressing their perceptions of their UE experiences. Scorecards are used in nontraditional, event-centered interventions as well as longer-term interventions, such as

**Table 2. Financial measures of bottom-line results.**

| Type of Measure | How Measured | Results Assumptions |
|---|---|---|
| **Business results** *(Level 4)* | A Level 4 measure generally is determined by identifying key business performance results prior to and after participants' UE development experiences. | The measure rests on the assumption that the UE experience is a key factor being used by business units to generate tangible business consequences identified through a thorough front-end analysis of the performance situation. |
| **ROI** *(Level 5)* | Level 5 measurement is simply an extension of Level 4 measurement. It compares the business results achieved through use of the UE development experience (the Level 4 measures) with the training costs incurred by the business units. Thus, Level 5 data report the monetary value of business results compared with the monetary costs of the HPI solution. | Sprint's business unit executives generally expect, and rightfully so, that for every one dollar invested in HPI, more than one dollar of benefit is earned. |

organization development projects or executive coaching. In addition to questions about the consultants' methods, behaviors and effectiveness, these scorecards ask managers and executives to give their perceptions of the dollar value of the interventions. All of the results data is displayed on the intranet *UE Pulse.* Scorecard participants are asked if they believe significant bottom-line results have been achieved, and if so, the degree of confidence they have in the results. Identified as "perceptual ROI" (and very similar to what some people refer to as return-on-expectations or ROE), this data is collected but not displayed with calculated ROI data. Table 3, scorecard results from earlier in the year, shows the average perceptions of different kinds of products/services based on a seven-point scale. As with Level 1 data, employees and customers may pull this data at any time, but very little of it is pushed to anyone except under special circumstances. Perceptual ROI data is not included in this sample.

## Criteria for Bottom-Line Dollar Results and ROI Projects

One of the most important aspects of any search for bottom-line dollar results and ROI is to identify appropriate criteria for selecting projects. Pick the wrong projects, and failure is almost

# Table 3. Scorecard results.

| UE Function Group Product/Service Provider | 2000 Mean/Count | 2001 Mean/Count | 1Q02 Mean/Count | 2002 YTD Mean/Count |
|---|---|---|---|---|
| Customer relationship management consulting | 6.78/3 | 6.39/6 | 6.30/19 | 6.30/19 |
| Performance solutions/development | 6.54/27 | 6.71/73 | 6.62/35 | 6.62/35 |
| Research and evaluation | Began using scorecard in 2001 | 6.52/11 | No data reported/0 | No data reported/0 |
| Supplier management | 6.44/3 | 6.47/5 | No data reported/0 | No data reported/0 |
| UE IT/IS consulting | 6.67/3 | 6.63/7 | No data reported/0 | No data reported/0 |
| Assessment centers | 5.82/160 | 6.15/196 | 5.47/10 | 5.47/10 |
| Executive academy | Began using scorecard in 2001 | 5.83/84 | 5.77/22 | 5.77/22 |
| Executive coaching | 6.03/83 | 6.35/162 | 6.29/49 | 6.29/49 |
| Group debrief | Began using scorecard in 2001 | 6.43/10 | 6.44/3 | 6.44/3 |
| Project personnel | Began using scorecard in 2001 | 6.39/82 | 6.09/20 | 6.09/20 |
| Transitional coaching | Began using scorecard in 2001 | 5.40/5 | 1.83/2 | 1.83/2 |
| Other delivery | Began using scorecard in 2001 | 7.0/1 | No data reported/0 | No data reported/0 |

guaranteed. At the UE, the criteria are quite simple and are adhered to rather closely. There are three major hurdles:

1.  The first criterion is simply, is there a value proposition? By "value proposition" we mean how does the target audience performance addressed in this proposed initiative directly affect the bottom line? Does the target audience add revenue that tracks to the bottom line? Produce savings that track to the bottom line? Avoid costs that would otherwise track to the bottom line? If there is not a clear connection of the target population performance to the bottom line, there is generally no clear value proposition, and the initiative is not at all a likely candidate for measurement.

2.  If there is a clear value proposition, the next criterion is how does the customer measure the connection from the target population to the bottom line? Access to that measurement system is certainly a requirement, but the UE would generally expect the customer to conduct the actual measurement(s). If there is no current measurement method(s), it is not a likely candidate for bottom-line measurement. The UE is not really in the business of measuring customer processes. If developing a customer measurement system really needs to be part of the project, it can be done, but such work would increase project scope and cost substantially.

3.  If there is a direct measurement system of the value proposition, the UE looks at reasons to expend the extra effort for the particular project: Does it represent a large expenditure or a large part of the business unit's budget? Is it strategically significant to the customer? Is it important in enhancing the UE relationship with this customer? Does it have a potential for unusually positive results? Is it needed for proof of concept of a new technology?

If the project gets to this hurdle and the answer to any of these questions is affirmative, then it is a good candidate for a bottom-line value measurement.

## Training Scorecard Application

To understand the UE value measurement process more fully, it may be useful to review one human performance improvement project in depth. Remember that terminology is not standard in the field of HRD. What Sprint refers to as a scorecard is the customer feedback reports to the UE. The methodology described in this section is what Sprint refers to simply as UE reporting.

The accounts receivable measurement (ARM New Hire Program) project is particularly interesting because of its multiple sources of bottom-line results and the promise it demonstrates for future UE work in the general area of call centers. Only the name, locations, and phone numbers connected with the project are modified here to protect identities; all the numerical data is presented as reported on the actual project.

## Project Background

Let us begin with some basic information: The ARM project takes place in an accounts receivable call center with over 100 representatives taking largely inbound calls from customers not up-to-date on their telephone bill payments. The customers calling in are doing so because they have typically just received notice that they are seriously delinquent in paying their bills and that they should call 1.800.XXX.XXXX to avoid the loss of service. Accounts receivable representatives (AR reps) are expected to make specific arrangements to collect the overdue amounts. Those arrangements and subsequent customer actions are then tracked with the positive expectation that customers will pay their phone bills and remain loyal Sprint customers. In other words, the AR reps have a very tough job to do! They deal with customers who are generally unhappy from the outset. In many cases, customers who have not paid their phone bills are going through difficult times at work or at home, and this situation adds to their stress. In some cases, customers are legitimately upset with Sprint because they paid— or thought they paid—their bills already.

Prior to the ARM project, new AR reps received a seven-week training course and a big AR practices book (with a large online database) before going to work in the call center. It would take them several months to ramp up to full performance, with a lot of formal and informal coaching by trainers, supervisors, and colleagues. Frustration levels among AR reps at this location were generally high, and collection results were not meeting quotas. To improve performance and thus reduce training costs, the UE partnered with this ARM call center on a pilot training program, initially with a group of eight newly hired AR reps.

## The *New* New Hire Program

The ARM New Hire Training Program was cut from seven to four weeks and focused more on working with people and becoming comfortable with the equipment. The previous curriculum had focused more on specific methods, procedures, practices, and requirements. (According to many call center people, all of that was forgotten before new reps got to the floor.) Rather than expecting the new reps to remember so much of the material, trainers supplied them with an overlaid electronic performance support system (EPSS) and trained them to use it. The overlaid program Sprint uses is called the UE Guide. According to the UE Guide product manager, Alicja Towster, "It is rather like having a private coach available at all times."

Nearly all AR reps' work is conducted on the phone and at a computer station. When a customer calls in, the rep finds the customer information and then follows a procedure designed to engage the customer in committing to a reasonable and responsible plan of action to maintain his or her account. If the AR rep does not remember exactly what goes in what field on the customer account screen, he or she has to look it up. In the past, this meant finding the right page in the big, thick user manual or searching the extensive online database, and then hoping what was found was correct and up-to-date. Sometimes, the rep could find the information relatively quickly, but frequently it took some time—more than just a few seconds—with an upset customer becoming more upset during the delay. Other times, the rep would take several minutes or remember incorrectly, and thus cause confusion and rework on that call, and create the need for yet another call at a later date.

The UE Guide changed all of that. To a user, the UE Guide solution is quite simple but wholly comprehensive. No matter which screen field the AR reps are working with, all they have to do is drag and drop a single icon to get the information they want about that field: What is the purpose of collecting the information? What detail is needed? How should they ask follow-up questions to get the needed response? How much is the sales tax in Altamonte Springs, Florida, or Gaylord, Minnesota? A script can be provided in English and Spanish (UE Guide accommodates other languages in other locations as well). The AR reps do not need to think of their own questions. They simply focus on what they are trying to accomplish while treating the customer pleasantly. In general, the people who use the system like it very much, and this was reflected in very high Level 1 evaluation results. The initial pilot scores averaged 6.65 on a 7-point scale.

### The Results of the Project

UE people on the project felt Level 1 results were superb! Because this was a pilot, Level 1 evaluations also included daily plus/delta reviews, loaded with plusses, and provided excellent feedback for improving the product. Development associates used focus groups and individual interviews to collect data, too, and this data was consistently positive among newly hired employees. All of the Level 1 data showed that AR rep new hires were very pleased with essentially all aspects of the training.

Level 2 results were informal but myriad, as the key developer and the instructor remained on site for several weeks to identify any glitches in the software or other problems that might arise. They also were there to provide coaching, but found that little was needed. Their observations continued over a period of several weeks. They worked extensively with supervisors, helping them become comfortable in coaching on the technology. The highly experienced UE education consultant team comprised a performance solutions developer and subject matter expert for call centers who provided the overall design for the curriculum, an education consultant who facilitated the sessions, and two developers who contributed to programming the UE Guide EPSS. One of the developers also facilitated follow-up focus group sessions and interviews.

Level 3 results also were abundant because each time an AR rep requests UE Guide assistance, the hit is recorded automatically. In the UE, we refer to the EPSS as an example of blurring the line between learning and work. The data shows that hits have reduced rather rapidly from a level suggesting almost continuous use to a level depicting occasional use. This data suggests that participants are learning from the UE Guide solution quite effectively and working more effectively as they use it on the job.

Levels 4 and 5 results were perhaps the most impressive of all! The total customer cost for developing the UE Guide and curriculum came to $216,587. An initial ROI of $870,000 resulted from the AR reps moving out of the classroom and onto the phones full time three weeks before they would have done so using the old curriculum. Figure 5, the UE value measurement summary, describes this project, so you may wish to refer to it for all of the information summarized there. Although the initial $870,000 return was quite positive, it was not the most significant part of the bottom-line results in this project and is not identified in figure 5. The really valuable part came from the productivity increases that pilot participants achieved. On an annualized basis, those eight people showed an increase of more than $5 million in collections over their experienced counterparts.

The data above the shaded line in figure 5 typically is completed when the project begins or shortly thereafter. When the project is completed, the costs and benefits fields are filled in and the system calculates the bottom-line results and ROI. Then that data automatically populates the ROI project log (figure 6). The UE market research manager provided the computer skills and, perhaps more important, the idea and the energy to automate this system. Prior to her contribution, there were numerous unconnected logs, summaries, and case

# Figure 5. UE value measurement summary.

| | |
|---|---|
| Business Unit | Xxxxxxxx Accounts Receivable Xxxxxxxx Call Center |
| Project Name | ARM New Hire Program |
| Project ID | Pilot Course # 09XXX |
| UE Solution Tool(s) | Blended: Instructor-led and UE Guide EPSS |
| Number of Users | Eight in pilot |
| Situation | New AR reps take seven weeks' classroom, then expected to perform on the job in complex and difficult situations with slow/nonpaying customers. Frustration levels high and collection results below quota. |
| Action | Redesigned the curriculum to reduce training by three weeks, and introduced UE Guide EPSS solution for continuing on the job learning and reinforcement of prior learning. |
| Value Proposition | Multiple value propositions: Increased revenue production with AR reps on the job three weeks earlier, increased daily revenue collection due to higher productivity. |
| Customer Contact | Marth Rxxxxx, (XXX) 501-XXXX |
| Customer Decision Support | Bill Pxxxxx, (816) 487-XXXX |
| UE Contacts | Jamie Kxxxxxx, (913) 906-XXXX; Jessica McXxxxxxxx, (913) 906-XXXX |
| Date ROI Project Identified | 01/14/02 |
| Date Detailed Evaluation Plan Established | 02/22/02 |
| Date to Evaluate | 05/31/02 |
| Date to Report Results | 06/14/02 |
| | |
| Calculated Results | In three-month trial period, pilot group achieved average daily revenue collection of $7,141.86 vs. $4,147.34 for incumbents, which annualizes to $5,301,682 in increased productivity. Not included: Collected $870,000 in first three weeks on the job. |
| Additional Benefits Not Yet Calculated | AR reps with UE Guide get customized, focused, always correct "coaching" just-in-time, while speaking with customers. Reduces call time somewhat, and unexpected increase in customer service. Buoys up AR rep morale enormously. |
| Outcome Comments | Incumbents have resisted UE Guide, said they didn't need it, but tested at 48 percent on same test pilot group averaged 99 percent. If incumbents = pilot productivity, annual increase greater than $70 million. |

| Costs (include development, travel expenses, salaries, etc.) | Benefits (increased revenues, decreased expenses, cost avoidance) | ROI (do not enter; will calculate automatically.) |
|---|---|---|
| $216,587 | $5,301,682 | 2348% |

study sheets requiring that all data be filled in multiple times. One of the most popular uses of the summaries occurs when UE representatives, particularly executives, prepare to meet with business unit customer executives. They simply scan the log and then print copies of the most current data on recent project summaries. UE executives find it very handy to bring themselves up-to-date on some good news in business units prior to meetings in which they expect to talk with business unit executives. They often take copies with them as reminders that silently communicate this message: "Here is what the UE has done for you recently."

Some of the summaries also were used in a presentation to a leadership development roundtable on the subject of ROI, sponsored by the Corporate Executive Board and hosted in Overland Park by Sprint's UE in June 2002. A number of chief learning officers (CLOs) attended from all over the country and the UE vice president was the host executive. Use of the summaries helped those CLOs immediately recognize the contribution the UE had made in the varied cases presented for discussion.

Many organizational leaders speak of their people as their most important asset. This project certainly demonstrates the enormous potential that people offer for positively affecting organizational performance when they are provided with the right tools and training!

## Communicating Results

This case study is focused on the Level 4 and Level 5 data calculated, reported, and communicated both within the UE and to its Sprint business unit customers. In contrast to the perceptual ROI data mentioned earlier, calculated bottom-line dollar results and ROI data are pushed to customers through customer relations management team members. This data is placed on the intranet at a site to which the business units have access so they also can pull the data. CRMT members frequently provide to executives and managers ad hoc informal reports of Level 4 and Level 5 results and produce more formal monthly or quarterly reports of UE support efforts. This ROI data is kept current on the intranet so reports can be pulled at any time. Figure 6 shows a portion of a partial, actual log in a Microsoft Excel format as it appears online (the only changes were made to protect anonymity). The UE value measurement summaries for each calculated ROI project, shown in figure 5, lead up to the project logs, with the case study data automatically populating the logs.

# Figure 6. ROI project log.

| | | | ROI Project Log | | | Nxxxxx Sxxxxxxx Group |
|---|---|---|---|---|---|---|
| **Business Unit** | **Project Name** | **Project ID** | **UE Medium** | **# of Users** | **Value Proposition** | |
| NSG, Field | XXX Boot Camp | NSG # 1XX | Instructor-Led | 40 annually | Reduced cost to Field Operations through reducing travel costs for participants. Using a minimum of instructor-led training with an emphasis on UE Live virtual classroom, self-directed training using CD, and UE Guide to provide on-the-job follow-up. | |
| Pxxxxxxxxxx | ABCD Program Guide | Performance Support | UE Guide | 350-1500 | Increased productivity, reduced errors, and reduced rework through EPSS system rather than having to refer to large manual with continuous changes. | |
| NSG Help Desk | XXXX introduction | Pilot Course # 14XXX | UE Live virtual classroom | 800 | Primary value proposition is savings of travel expenses and less time lost from work. | |
| NSG Mxxxxx-Xxxxxx Xxxxx | Pricing Tool Introduction | XXX-0314 | XXX Tool | 400 | Increased productivity, reduced errors, and reduced rework through use of XXX Pricing Tool, enabling instant bundling pricing. | |
| NSG Bxxxxxx Dxxx | XYZ Instrument Consulting | 0 | CRMT Consulting | 6 people in a newly reorganized unit | Productivity gains for the 6 team members, tuition savings due to cutting out a small part of a $600 course. | |
| NSG | Leadership Development Program | LDP Curriculum | CRMT consulting, UE course demand sessions | 573 | Saved T&E expenses by putting training into one module rather than 2. Saved additional T&E expenses by reducing course time by one day, from 3 to 2. | |
| NSG, Field | EVA in Field Xxxxxxxx | 0 | e-learning | 50 | Savings to the bottom line due to making financially desirable decisions. | |

| Date ROI Project ID'd | Date Eval Plan Establ'd | Date to Evaluate | Date to Report Results | Total Benefit Less Cost | ROI | Calculated Results |
|---|---|---|---|---|---|---|
| 01/30/02 | 02/14/02 | 08/02/02 | 08/16/02 | $ - | #DIV/0! | 0 |
| 04/30/02 | 07/31/02 | 10/11/02 | 01/00/00 | $ - | #DIV/0! | 0 |
| 02/14/02 | 02/14/02 | 02/22/02 | 02/28/02 | $ 100,060.00 | 1345% | Calculated only savings travel expense and time lost from work. Have not yet determined value of accomplishing training in abbreviated time period, shortening overall roll-out of new system. |
| 03/20/02 | 03/20/02 | 04/09/02 | 04/09/02 | $810,000.00 | 7082% | Increased sales attributed to use of the XXX Pricing Tool. Want to use for the Lxxxxx-Mxxxxxx Xxxxx, too. |
| 01/17/02 | 04/24/02 | 04/24/02 | 05/06/02 | $ 12,601.00 | 1680% | Calculated benefits of completing report 30 days early, plus savings on tuition, but only $750 in consulting costs. |
| 03/07/02 | 04/16/02 | 06/28/02 | 07//09/02 | $ 266,829.00 | 5337% | Calculated T&E expenses, saved more than estimated since not all travelers rented cars, but car-pooled to some degree. |
| 01/30/02 | 01/00/00 | 01/00/00 | 01/00/00 | $ - | #DIV/0! | Dropped in February. Customer lost interest, apparently. |
| | | | | $2,089,490.00 | | |

## Lessons Learned

Although it might be nice to say that at Sprint we did everything right the first time, some of us actually learned a number of lessons the hard way. For example, I must admit that I experienced some of the lessons several times before full learning took place. We will review just a few lessons that I feel might be most useful to others. Some of the earlier lessons concerned internal UE matters. Some of the later lessons applied more to customers. Most of the lessons learned have corollaries for both internal and customer groups, even if they are not specifically described that way here.

- *Involve the people involved.* It is frequently not convenient to gather all the thoughts and ideas of the group of people taking part in a specific issue prior to designing a new process. There is often a rush for results, a push for reaching milestones, for making things happen. On the other hand, there is no substitute for early involvement of those who are expected to carry out a project or process. Push the scales toward *more* rather than a balanced approach or less in terms of people involvement.

- *Get help from the most experienced SME(s).* It is much easier for the SME manager to assign rookies to your project because they have more available time, but getting the real SMEs, the experts, fully involved *before* making critical decisions is essential. I have found, without exception, that doing so has saved more time and effort in repairing errors, misconceptions, and even blatant hostility than making decisions without full input from the appropriate "others." Generally, people will spend a lot more time fighting a poor decision, inappropriate process step, faulty process, and so forth than it would have taken to consult them and do it right the first time.

- *Involve the right people.* Sometimes it is difficult to see who the "right" people are because so many people are involved in the work of a corporate university. In starting a bottom-line measurement and ROI function, it is tempting to start out by planning the measurement department to-be. The first planning should determine the appropriate people to involve in measurement. They may be people already in the organization, not in a new department.

- *Start effective measurement with communications between the executives paying the bills and the university.* The UE can only be effective if it provides the appropriate strategic solutions to development issues. Managers and SMEs may know all about the details of the work, but only executives know why they are willing to spend several hundred thousand dollars on a training program. At the UE, this means the CRMT needs to talk with those executives and ensure that they really know the right answers to key questions: Why? How will the executive recognize success? How should the project really be measured? What are the measures that really count? CRMT members are tasked with creating and maintaining executive relationships, so they—rather than someone from the measurement department—must be the ones to communicate up front with executives about what they really expect.

- *Recognize the magnitude of the change.* It may sound simple to introduce a dollar-value measurement focus to a corporate university—after all, ROI is built around a pretty simple algebraic equation—but the real change is not simple. The real change involves altering the basic way many people look at their jobs. It adjusts how people gain their work satisfaction. It is a major, transformational organization development issue reaching deep into the organization and affecting how people think about their work. It is not going to be accomplished in the short time it might take just to introduce the mechanics of the dollar-value measurement formula for computing ROI. It is, *at the very least,* a multiyear effort requiring support and advocacy at all levels based on *why* the change is important to the corporate university. The support and advocacy must become literal leadership behaviors with executives and managers *using* the results of bottom-line measurements as part of organizational management after the initial introductory period is over. That is the point at which the real change begins—not when it is completed—although that recognition may not align with the expectations of all leaders.
- *Be consistent.* When some early-adopter UE employees balked at using the "standard" ROI formula of "([benefits − costs]/costs) × 100 = ROI%," I introduced other measures, such as the benefits-to-costs ratio, "benefits/costs = X:1." Through that experiment, I found that ratios were easier to understand and percentage measures were awkward to express when numbers became large, as they frequently do in HRD projects. Then I introduced what I called ROI ratios, computed as "benefits − costs/costs = X:1," the same equation as *net* benefit/cost ratio. It was a good idea with great intentions, but it did not work. I finally learned not to change things like the equation for measuring dollar return-on-investment. It confuses people and may reduce UE credibility with accountants. It probably does not matter what method you adopt if you are consistent and call it by its most nearly correct name, even though there may be some flexibility in what various measures are called. Talk to your accounting and finance colleagues about what they call the measure(s).

- *Always count on accounting/finance people as your friends.* And *always* get them involved in what you are doing early in each project. They know a lot about the measures available and where to get them. They are likely to know what measures are really important and what measures are less so. Working with accountants may feel a little intimidating for HRD professionals not accustomed to using and creating accounting data, but remember that accountants are people, too. Let them know what you are trying to accomplish, show them how you want to do it, then ask for their help. Accountants are trained to look at things carefully, to seek factual information, so expect them to ask some tough questions and not immediately jump on the bandwagon. If they see you are serious and mean well—even if they do not agree with all of your methods—they will almost always join with you if you give them a chance. They often have the ears of customer executives. Like those executives, if they do not know what you are doing in terms of developing bottom-line dollar results and ROI, they will undoubtedly be skeptical, perhaps to the point of acting against what should be your mutual interests.
- *Create and communicate big-picture plans.* Write a white paper on your measurement plans and distribute it widely. Redistribute it as you make significant changes. Draw the process as a flowchart and distribute it. Always ask for feedback when sending out such materials. Listen to the feedback. Take every opportunity, including volunteering as a speaker, to talk to internal university work groups about what you are doing. Listen for people's interests and concerns. Build on the interests and deal with the concerns because others will have them too.
- *Be conservative with your claims.* Be careful to avoid claiming bottom-line dollar value for things that customers might feel are the result of their own work. If value can be viewed both in a conservative way and in an optimistic way, take the conservative stance and mention the optimistic view, or let your customer come up with it. What looks to you like a low ROI percentage may look good to your customers. One of Sprint's projects resulted in an annualized ROI of 93 percent. (This may not be bad for a capital item, but it is very low for typical HRD work.) The customer was delighted! He was able to decide that he was going to do all of his training for that geographically dispersed group using this approach. The method made it possible for him to attend virtually every training session of the group, and he thought that was invaluable.
- *Be a partner with your customers.* Don't forget that there is no ROI without your customers. They make your job possible. They can do

without you, but you cannot do without them. Share the credit for your successes. The more you share the credit, the more credit there is, because goodwill and positive reinforcement are not zero-sum concepts. When there is a blend of training with capital expenditure and/or changed management practices, for example, try to view it as one project. Put all the costs together and measure all the results together. It is usually more valuable to spend your time working on the next project than quibbling over who gets credit for what percentage of the results. (And you will never get it exactly right, even if you achieve apparent consensus.) If your customer is insistent on dividing up the credit, do not spend a lot of time fighting it. Help the customer do it as equitably as is reasonable, then move on. When planning the next project with that customer, suggest trying it as a partnership rather than worrying about who gets what part of the credit. Maybe your customer will have learned something of value from the previous project. Finally, compliment the customers who are doing a good job. Trust me, they are not getting too much positive reinforcement already.

## Questions for Discussion

I hope that this case study stimulates a great deal of discussion—the more the better. Question the techniques, the problems, the successes cited, the lessons learned, the recommendations made. Additionally, you might consider some of the following questions for discussion:
1. What is the significance of the customer value proposition to HRD? What do you do if your customer is measuring "wrong" things, but not the value proposition?
2. What criteria should you use for determining which projects to choose to measure the bottom line?
3. Who are the people in your organization who should be leading the measurement effort, based on desired relationships with customer executives? How can you get them involved?
4. Should you use perceptual ROI or ROE in your organization? Would it enhance the perceived value of HRD contributions?
5. Who is responsible for bottom-line measurement of HRD initiatives—the HRD function or your customers? Who should do the study—HRD or the customers? Who should maintain the majority of the data?

## Final Words and Acknowledgments

Many people other than those mentioned in this chapter contributed greatly to the Sprint UE Value Measurement Process. Lois

Bany, keeper of *The Pulse,* was indispensable in providing data and graphics and in guiding me about the data. Bill Dichiser, Kevin Gabriel, and Susan Withrow from Decision Support made many of the details happen behind the scenes, without much notice or thanks. The UE market research manager who helped to bring all the documents into a form that actually worked was Patti Hanson. Developers Steve Robertson and Victoria Fouts turned ideas into an actual ARM New Hire Program, and performance solutions consultant Ina Friend and education consultant Minnie Robinson actually delivered and provided follow-up coaching and guidance. Surely there are deserving, hard-working people whom I have not mentioned here—I thank you and extend my humblest apologies.

UE vice president Sandy Price has been the real spark in pushing Sprint's University of Excellence to become more accountable to its customers, and in communicating to customer executives that they should expect more accountability for achieving their measures of performance. She recognized the need and has both pushed and pulled the UE associates toward a human performance improvement approach to their work. She has been relentless in continuing this effort for more than three years and still continues to smile through all of the difficulties and challenges she faces in the struggle to cause this organizational change. Steve Wright, director of technology planning and decision support in the UE, has been the sponsoring executive to supply the resources to make the UE's measurement program work. They are the two executives who demonstrated the insight and foresight to proceed and provided dogged ongoing support to make things happen. They led the efforts to turn the perspective of 600 UE associates from a traditional, educational view of the UE's function toward a more accountable, human performance improvement view. The dollar-value measurement project continues to be a major organizational change that likely would never even have been attempted without Price's leadership, vision, support, and personal efforts. The organizational change certainly is not complete. It is off to a good start. As of mid-2002, 55 projects of the sort described earlier are taking place, just slightly more than one year after the UE became formally focused on improving its value measurement process.

## The Author

Joel S. Finlay is a senior organization development consultant assigned to the Planning Group in Sprint's University of Excellence. He earned baccalaureate and master's degrees in organizational communication and a doctorate in management. His Ph.D. focused specifically on leadership effects in organizational change. He has worked at Sprint for more than five years, largely as an internal organization development consultant working with matters of change in the technology services function. Prior to coming to Sprint in 1997, he worked in both internal and external consulting positions, helping to improve performance and quality in more than 200 organizations, many of them *Fortune 500* companies in the United States, but also in Belgium, Canada, Central America, England, France, Iceland, Ireland, and Poland. In addition to his internal work at Sprint, he includes two other very distinguished external clients in his work, Malcolm Baldrige National Quality Award winners Zytec and Xerox. He also has worked with public sector clients, including the Department of Defense, the General Services Administration, and the National Aeronautics and Space Administration.

Finlay is a registered organization development consultant (RODC) by the Organization Development Institute (about 100 people worldwide hold this credential), where he also served on the board of directors for more than 10 years. He is a past editor of the *Organization Development Journal* and has written more than 50 articles, papers, presentations, book chapters, and books. He was recently honored as "Outstanding Researcher in Quality" and was profiled in *The International Who's Who in Quality*. He received a lifetime achievement award from the Heartland O.D. Group, the Midwest ODI-ODN Network. If you have questions, comments, or other information about which to contact him, please call 913.906.7582 for his office at Sprint, 913.706.4433 for PCS, or 913.906.7514 for facsimile, or reach him through email at joel.s.finlay@mail.sprint.com.

## References

Kirkpatrick, Donald L. (1959). Techniques for evaluating training programs. *Training and Development*, multiple issues.

Kirkpatrick, Donald L. (1994). *Evaluating Training Programs: The Four Levels.* San Francisco: Berrett Koehler.

Phillips, Jack J. (1997). *Handbook of Training Evaluation and Measurement Methods: Proven Models and Methods for Evaluating Any HRD Program.* 3rd ed. Boston: Butterworth-Heinemann.

# Six Levels of Training Evaluation: Improving Quality and Reducing Manufacturing Costs

## Analog Devices, Inc.

Mo Maghsoudnia and Lucy Strandberg

*Analog Devices, Inc. (ADI)—a manufacturer of silicon wafers located in Santa Clara, California, the heart of Silicon Valley—used a six-level training scorecard in conjunction with a performance-based training needs assessment and a best-in-class performance improvement system to advance a corporate strategy of cost reduction, product quality improvement, and adherence to work procedures. This case study, co-written by the operations manager and the training manager, describes how they applied the training scorecard to identify several cost reduction opportunities in their manufacturing operation. It also details how they got employees to follow work procedures precisely and to transform their team into a unified, results-oriented culture that was able to achieve significant cost reduction, improved quality, and increased employee morale while integrating their actions with management's overall production scorecard. This case study highlights how management can use a training scorecard and integrate it with the production scorecard.*

## Company Profile

Analog Devices, Inc. is a leader in the design, manufacturing, and marketing of high-performance analog, mixed-signal, and digital-signal processing (DSP) integrated circuits (ICs) used in signal processing applications. ADI's products are sold to a wide variety of customers in the communications, computer, consumer, and industrial markets. During FY2001, approximately 40 percent of ADI's revenues were derived from the industrial market, 38 percent from the

*This case was prepared to serve as a basis for discussion rather than to illustrate either effective or ineffective administrative and management practices.*

communications market, and the remaining 22 percent from the computer and consumer markets. ADI's products are sold to more than 60,000 customers worldwide through a direct salesforce, third-party industrial distributors, and independent sales representatives. The company has direct sales offices in 19 countries, including the United States. Approximately 39 percent of ADI's FY2001 revenues came from customers in North America, and most of the balance came from customers in Europe and Asia. The company is headquartered near Boston, in Norwood, Massachusetts, and has manufacturing facilities in Massachusetts, California, North Carolina, Ireland, the Philippines, Taiwan, and the United Kingdom. Founded in 1965, ADI employs approximately 8,800 people worldwide. The company's stock (NYSE: ADI) is included in the Standard & Poor's 500 Index. Sales for fiscal year 2001 were $2.8 billion. As of the fourth quarter of fiscal 2001, approximately 80 percent of total revenues came from analog products.

Signal processing is proceeding along a path to replace data processing as the primary growth driver for the semiconductor industry. There is little doubt that high-performance analog and DSP will be the enabling technologies at the heart of many of the semiconductor industry's highest growth opportunities over the next five to 10 years. ADI's DSP business has been gaining marketshare over the past few years and is poised for significant growth as the communications market recovers. ADI's DSP core road map is competitive, their vertical market penetration is strong in many emerging markets, and their ability to combine high-performance analog with DSP provides ADI an advantage with customers looking for total signal processing capability.

The ADI Santa Clara, California, plant has approximately 300 employees who manufacture silicon wafers that make up a wide variety of chips or ICs for both high-quality commercial applications and military/aeronautic use with increasingly stringent specification standards. The cultural factors at the plant include differing expectations and attitudes among operators, engineers, and maintenance personnel, as well as wide-ranging levels of education, which include formal education such as college and university training and nonformal education. The variety of personnel especially affected the responsiveness to the training scorecard Level 1 surveys. Management was interested in the broader picture of metrics and ROI; supervisors were concerned with the microlevel operations, such as the production schedule impact of pulling operators off the production line for training.

## Key Issues Prompting Training Scorecard Intervention

Cycle time, production line yield, rework rate, scrap, on-time delivery, and customer satisfaction are universal issues facing every management and operations team involved in high-tech manufacturing.

As background to these key issues one must understand the complexity of the wafer manufacturing process. To fit many hundreds of separate circuits onto a tiny chip of silicon about 5 mm$^2$ requires incredibly precise production techniques. The components in a chip's circuits are measured in microns (a thousandth of a millimeter) and must be positioned with an accuracy of one or two microns. Chips are made using sophisticated computer-controlled machinery in ultra-clean, particle-free environments. High-powered microscopes are used to inspect chips during the manufacturing process. To make a chip, the components and circuit connections are built up of 20 or more layers in and on the surface of silicon.

When the raw wafers reach the manufacturing process they are thoroughly cleaned and put into a red-hot oxidation furnace, where they grow a thin insulating layer of chemical called silicon dioxide. Then they are coated with a soft, light-sensitive polymer called photoresist. That and the next process are repeated for every circuit layer of the chip. Each wafer will make several hundred to several thousand chips, depending on the type of device being manufactured.

Using the circuit designs held in a computer's memory, a set of photomasks is made, one photomask for each layer of the chip. The masks are squares of glass on which the pattern of a circuit layer is printed by a technique called photolithography. The wafers are exposed against the photomask whereby the circuit pattern is printed on the wafer. At this point the wafer goes through typically up to 20 different masking layers with four different stages for each layer and with every stage containing a different process and the use of eight separate pieces of equipment. The glass masks, about 10 cm$^2$, hold the patterns for a few hundred chips side by side. What is vital to understand is that as each layer is made it is manually inspected and this inspection area is called Develop Inspect. In this ADI plant, Develop Inspect is human dependent, is done on a purely manual basis, and is the critical gauge or quality check of the photolithography process and all of the earlier manufacturing stages. This means that if a chip goes through 20 different masking layers, it then also goes through the Develop Inspect area 20 times, once for each layer.

Develop Inspect ensures that the resist image does not have defects, pattern deviations, misalignment of layers, exposure problems, residual resist, and so forth, and meets the quality criteria for the lithography process and the customer's criteria. It is critical at that stage to catch any wafer defects or deviations because, if caught, these wafers can be reworked and corrected. Any defects found after a wafer passes the Develop Inspect area cannot be reworked and the wafer would be scrapped. In such a case, there is a waste of one to four weeks of work or cycle time and 1 to 20 masking layers, depending on the stage in the process at which the error occurred. This waste and delay affects delivery time and customer satisfaction, as well as the cost of labor, materials, time, and employee morale. Additionally, if defects are not being caught at Develop Inspect, it is not possible to correct the root causes of the defects that are occurring in the earlier stages of manufacturing.

The application of a training scorecard was envisioned to enable the reduction of scrap and rework and thereby reduce the cost of quality by freeing up resources for more vital production activities. Rework and scrap delays new lots coming in and, more important, affects the overall line yield, which in turn affects the overall cost of operation. If yield is lower than capacity as a result of rework and scrap, available capacity is being used up, and if there is more product demand than capacity, the company is forced to spend more capital for more equipment or manufacturing space to meet the capacity demands.

## Training Scorecard Methodology

A training scorecard was implemented to translate ADI's corporate strategy into a comprehensive set of performance measures to ensure that training aligned with ADI's strategic short- and long-term business issues, including cost reduction, quality improvement, and increased employee morale. The training scorecard enabled management to measure the effectiveness of training. It increased training's accountability by measuring on six levels and by measuring employee morale and financial return-on-investment (ROI) based on metric improvement results. Figure 1 shows the training scorecard model used. The various levels of the model are explained below:

- *Level 0*—This level used a performance and metric-based assessment developed by Dr. Trude Fawson, nationally recognized speaker on practical approaches to training and human performance, to determine who should be trained and what the training content should be.
- *Levels 1-4* used the model developed by Donald L. Kirkpatrick (1998).
- *Level 1*—What is the employee's opinion of the training?

**Figure 1. ADI's training scorecard.**

| | AREAS AND METRICS | | | | | | INTANGIBLES | | | |
|---|---|---|---|---|---|---|---|---|---|---|
| | Develop Inspect | | LTO | New Device Process | Novellus Checksheet Team | | Combined Results for All Areas | | | |
| | Escapes Scrap | Workers Retained and Certified (%) | Scrap | Scrap by Human Error | Step 3 Check Scrap | Total Scrap | Employee Morale | Employee Evaluation | Employee Proficiency (%) | Skill Transfer to Job (%) |
| Level 0 Goal | | | | | | | | | | |
| Baseline | | | | | | | | | | |
| Level 1 Goal | | | | | | | | | | |
| Achieved | | | | | | | | | | |
| Level 3 Goal | | | | | | | | | | |
| Achieved | | | | | | | | | | |
| Level 4 Achieved | | | | | | | | | | |
| Level 5 Achieved | | | | | | | | | | |

- *Level 2*—Are trainees fully proficient in what they have been taught?
- *Level 3*—Have skills transferred from training to the job as verified by the employee's supervisor?
- *Level 4*—What are the results in improved metrics, such as productivity, quality, cycle time, costs, and revenue?
- *Level 5*—What is the ROI, based on the ROI model developed by Jack J. Phillips (1997)?

Additional scorecard intangibles included employee morale, supervisor involvement, personal commitment to "doing it right the first time," and personal pride.

## Training Scorecard Application

Based on management's strategy of reducing cost, improving quality, and increasing employee morale, a Level 0 performance-based needs assessment was conducted. The training scorecard Level 0 evaluation uncovered significant scrap reduction opportunities in four vital areas of the plant. If handled effectively, these opportunities would cause a chain reaction of metric improvement on such issues as cycle time, production line yield, rework rate, on-time delivery, and customer satisfaction.

Scrap resulting from employee error was identified as the significant metric to affect with training. Teams driven by operations in coordination with the training manager evaluated each process using Pareto charts and total quality management (TQM) tools of Plan-Do-Check-Act. That endeavor identified four target production areas. Scrap metrics were collected as a baseline against which to compare and measure training results, and the various devices and lots being scrapped were given a dollar value in coordination with the finance department.

Four key areas were chosen and the following teams were organized: the Develop Inspect Metric Team, the LTO (low-temperature oxide) Scrap Reduction Team, the New Device Process Team, and the Novellus Checklist Team.

- *Develop Inspect*—The training scorecard Level 0 identified the Develop Inspect area as a critical station in the overall process that could be addressed strategically with training. This area was experiencing significant scrap and the Develop Inspect Metric Team was chartered to reduce scrap by 50 percent. A project plan was developed by which scrap data was gathered. Existing processes and specifications were analyzed and the method of training was evaluated.

- *LTO*—This plant area also was generating scrap as a result of the loading process, mixed lots, and input of recipe procedures, and the LTO Scrap Reduction Team was mandated to cut to zero the amount of scrap produced by human error. Up to this time, trainers used specifications without any guidance to train operators, and operators were not attaining full proficiency.
- *New Device Process*—This plant area operates on a complex software program and scrap was produced by human error, such as sequencing mistakes and lack of proficiency in operating the program. The goal set for this area was zero scrap.
- *Novellus*—This area of the plant is similar to the LTO process that applies an oxide film onto wafers. Lack of proficiency in selecting and applying a wide array of recipes to a complexity of processes made this area susceptible to scrap production, although this step in the process is highly automated. Nevertheless, scrap was being produced due to a lack of proficiency in this area. A zero-scrap goal was set for this area.

The training scorecard Level 0 assessment included identifying flaws in the work procedures/specifications that did not align with the processes. Discrepancies were found between what the specifications required and what the operators were doing. In the Develop Inspect area, operators were using a five-point inspection plan, whereas the specifications required a nine-point inspection. The specifications also were evaluated against the process flow to ensure that the flow aligned with the actual procedures.

Who should be trained on what content was specified to include work procedure and specification revisions to align with processes and instructional design modules called "checksheets." At the initial level, Pareto charts were used to analyze operator error in comparison with process error and equipment error. The human error factor turned out to be the largest opportunity for improvement and cost reduction. On the next level, Pareto charts were used to identify the root cause of the human error so that training could be targeted strategically to remedy the cause.

Level 1 evaluation surveys of the training were conducted through a printed questionnaire. Trainees were asked how they liked the training, what they learned, and what improvements could be made. Surveys also were conducted to determine the effectiveness of the new work process, the training and support materials, and the quality of the training. Trainers received solicited and unsolicited feedback about the training effectiveness.

Level 2 evaluations were done by way of trainer checkouts on work procedures/specifications to ensure full proficiency every step of the way.

Level 3 evaluations were done by line supervisors who were trained in the proficiency training system and then kept written logs and ensured that employees were "doing it right" on the job. Trainers observed trainees over a weeklong period after they signed off on their training modules to further ensure skill transfer.

Level 4 evaluations were based on the baseline metrics identified in the Level 0 evaluation and monitored throughout the training cycle, and on comparison metrics kept on a quarterly basis as a follow-up to the training cycle. Reduction of scrapped lots and scrapped wafers was monitored.

Level 5 evaluation was done by calculating the costs of implementing the training system against the metric decrease in scrap converted to dollars in coordination with the finance department.

## Training Program Description
### Historical Development

ADI decided to use the 100% Proficiency training system developed by Effective Training Solutions (ETS), a Silicon Valley-based performance improvement and consulting firm. Through years of research with high-tech manufacturers and government agencies, ETS found that traditional classroom or on-the-job training methods were achieving only mediocre levels of workforce proficiency, especially in fast-paced, rapid-change environments. It was also found that this proficiency gap was responsible for such things as human error, scrap, rework, and customer dissatisfaction. Even more basic problems were inadequate work procedures and specifications, and employees' inability to understand them fully and follow them correctly. To bridge this gap ETS set a benchmark for 100 percent proficiency defined as that point at which employees
- have all of the knowledge necessary to do their job(s)
- work fast and error free
- understand and follow work procedures precisely
- can exercise good judgment within the scope of their job(s).

The 100% Proficiency training system is based on research conducted by L. Ron Hubbard in the 1960s and published as a lecture series titled "The Key to Effective Learning Lectures" (Hubbard, 2002). This research showed that verbal training did not achieve full proficiency and that retention was very low after classroom training. It also showed that training was much more effective if organized on a supervised, self-paced basis to take into account learners' different learning styles and speeds.

## Intervention Type

Structured around a performance- and metric-based needs assessment, a performance improvement system called 100% Proficiency training was used as the intervention tool and a train-the-trainer approach was employed. All work procedures and specifications were reviewed and revised to match the processes and actions called for on each job function. Then all employees underwent a rigorous "Learning How to Learn" program that helped them learn to understand and follow work procedures and specifications without deviation and gave them the tools to achieve good judgment and accuracy on the job. Additionally, training modules called "checksheets" were used in conjunction with the work procedures and specifications.

Those checksheets provided a road map for the trainees to follow, laying out an exact sequence of steps, including study of work specifications and other documents and diagrams or visual aides and practical exercises to orient them to procedures, equipment, programs, and work applications. The checksheets also require employees to drill with hands-on practice during training rather than after training with live product on the job.

The target training population consisted of 34 inspectors in the Develop Inspect area, 12 operators in the LTO area, 10 operators in the New Device area, and 14 operators in the Novellus area located at the Santa Clara facility. The teams were charged to reduce scrap and thereby produce a financial return-on-investment and an expected payback period of four months.

## Prerequisites

Leadership commitment was a vital aspect of the success of this program, along with significant favorable estimated ROI potential demonstrated before the program was implemented and a highly qualified project manager assigned to implement and coordinate operations according to a project plan and timeline.

## Uniqueness of the Program

The component parts of the 100% Proficiency training system are the use of a six-level training scorecard and the integration of the system with management's production scorecard for strategic alignment with business goals. Another key element is the revision of specifications and work procedures written to a standard that achieves 100 percent proficiency. Operators/employees are trained on how to learn to full proficiency so that they are able to understand and follow work procedures precisely—a situation that creates self-reliance and increases employee morale.

The instructional design modules (checksheets) are primarily learner-centered, supervised, self-paced training modules based on the revised and accurate work procedures. They shift responsibility for and control of learning to the student. The student changes from a passive learner being lectured to or "talked at" to an active and interactive learner.

Standards of training are set to achieve 100 percent proficiency and the supervised and self-paced learning system increases confidence and reduces both training time and trainer time. The trainer doesn't explain—instead, he or she refers the trainee to the specifications or work procedures. Thus, the employee learns to comprehend fully and rely on the written specifications and work instructions rather than on verbal instruction, explanations, or opinions from co-workers. In this way, the role of the trainer shifts to coaching and quality assurance.

Supervisors are involved heavily at the front end of the training program to ensure skill transfer (Level 3), followed by the Level 4 and Level 5 training scorecard assessments that make training accountable for metric performance improvement.

## Program Content

The program comprises a series of training workshops, including an executive seminar for management that covers strategic alignment and use of the training scorecard and the 100% Proficiency training system so as to deploy it strategically to achieve business goals and metrics; a specification/work procedure writing workshop for content experts; supervisor training—to ensure that they maintain the 100 percent standard and verify skill transfer and metric improvement; a checksheet writer's workshop that teaches instructional designers how to write 100% Proficiency instructional modules; learning-how-to-learn workshops for trainees; coaching skills training for line trainers; and job-specific knowledge and skills training for operators. These workshops and training modules were delivered over a span of 16 weeks and the program was measured over a period of four quarters.

## Expected Results

The following results were expected from this program:

- an effective training scorecard aligned with the management performance scorecard
- a training scorecard system that is sustainable and effective for the long term
- elimination of errors resulting from human performance
- operators achieving 100 percent proficiency on their jobs
- improved employee morale
- significantly enhanced financial ROI
- notably increased supervisor involvement.

### Relationship to Other Programs

The operations manager chose to use the TQM Plan-Do-Check-Act methodology using quality teams to integrate with the training scorecard and the proficiency training. Teams were chartered to focus on applying those TQM tools to reduce scrap production.

## Training Program Results

Figure 2 presents the results of the training program. What follows is a discussion of the findings.

### Level 1

Level 1 results were excellent overall per survey. Among Level 1 surveys on administration of the checksheet, the training scorecard tool makes it possible to see the concentration (patterns) of low scores and high scores. For example, training time was typically rated 3, and one respondent actually rated it 1. A person wrote that everyone was required to be certified on the checksheet in two weeks and that wasn't enough time. Another person said he needed four to five weeks to do it properly. A pattern of specification quality or readability also came up as an issue, and although improvements were seen, more improvement was needed. Other comments made about upholding the standard of full proficiency pointed out the importance of using the training scorecard Level 1 as a tool for identifying weak points and areas needing further investigation so that corrective action could be taken.

### Level 2

Learning was guaranteed to be at a level of 100 percent proficiency, based on the successful completion of instructional modules, or checksheets. Practical drills and exercises and final checkouts by trainers guaranteed that employees were following work procedures and specifications with precision, accuracy, and speed.

# Figure 2. ADI's training scorecard results.

| | AREAS AND METRICS | | | | | | INTANGIBLES — Combined Results for All Areas | | | |
| | Develop Inspect | | | LTO | New Device Process | Novellus Checksheet Team | | | | |
| | Escapes Scrap per Quarter | Workers Retained and Certified (%) | Scrap per Work Week | Scrap by Human Error per Work Week | Step 3 Check Scrap per Quarter | Total Scrap per Quarter | Employee Morale | Employee Evaluation | Employee Proficiency (%) | Skill Transfer to Job (%) |
|---|---|---|---|---|---|---|---|---|---|---|
| Level 0 Measure | REDUCE BY 50% | 100% | 0 | 0 | 0 | 0 | Improve | | | |
| Baseline | 313 wafers | 30% | 61 wafers | 47 wafers | 43 wafers | 72 wafers | | | | |
| Level 1 Measure | | | | | | | | Scale 1-5 | | |
| Achieved | | | | | | | | 4.75 | | |
| Level 3 Goal | | | | | | | | | | 100% |
| Achieved | | | | | | | | | | 100% |
| Level 4 Achieved | REDUCED BY 58.3% 111 wafers | 100% | 3 wafers | REDUCED BY 94.9% 0 wafers | 0 wafers | REDUCED BY 65.9% 0 wafers | Improved | | | |
| Level 5 Achieved | 363% | | | 562% | | 260% | | | | |

## Level 3

Employees were demonstrating 100 percent proficiency on the job with complete skill transfer. Level 3 surveys were filled out by two supervisors—one night-shift supervisor and one day-shift supervisor. At a glance, their responses make it possible to discern strengths and shortcomings of the training for the implementation manager to investigate as appropriate.

One supervisor preferred this system of training because it "holds the trainee accountable" and "provides consistent training across all shifts." The Level 3 survey yielded a recommendation for operators to be trained on performing a specific process called Fab process audits (on which they normally would not have been trained)—a recommendation that could yield further data to improve the root-cause analysis for further scrap reduction.

The second-shift supervisor reported that the checksheets could be used even more effectively to uphold the full proficiency standard. This response added to the continuous improvement process and increased the quality and integrity of the training.

## Level 4 Metric Improvement

The areas targeted for scrap reduction using the 100% Proficiency system showed results that were immediate, dramatic, and most notably, *continued* to improve *after* the training was complete.

## Develop Inspect

The training achieved the goal by reducing human-error scrap 58.3 percent with a 363 percent ROI within three months. The largest target area for scrap was Develop Inspect where everyone was retrained on 100% Proficiency checksheets while meeting rising production demands. The scrap rate dropped in half that quarter and continued to drop the following two quarters, improving by 56 percent, 63.3 percent, and 63.7 percent, respectively, relative to the baseline.

Low scrap rates continued despite later uncertainties prompted by the economic downturn. On the Pareto charts that display sources of scrap, human error now falls consistently after equipment and process errors. Other significant benefits include reduced cycle time and improved line yield, increased morale, and reduced cost of quality and rework. Figure 3 illustrates the decrease in scrap produced in the third quarter compared with the previous three quarters. Figure 4 presents the time line for the 34 inspectors being retrained and recertified. Figure 5 depicts the decrease in scrap as the inspectors were recertified.

**Figure 3. Scrap produced in the third quarter compared with the previous four quarters.**

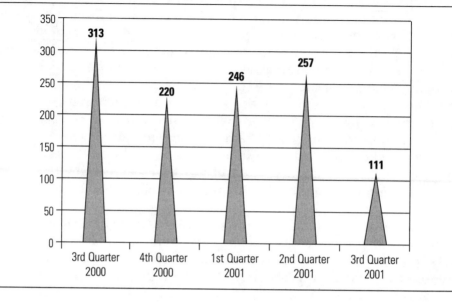

**Figure 4. Time line for the 34 inspectors being retrained and recertified.**

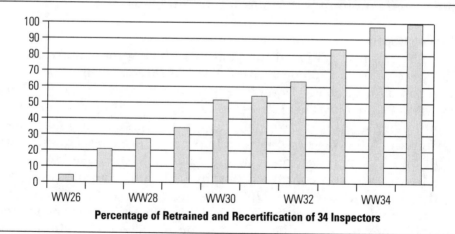

**Figure 5. Scrap decrease as inspectors were recertified.**

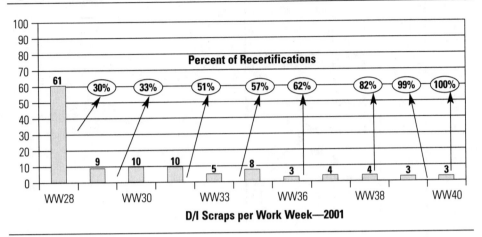

D/I Scraps per Work Week—2001

## LTO

Training virtually achieved the goal of zero scrap goal resulting from human performance problems. Improvement was 94.9 percent, with a 562 percent ROI, within two months. Figure 6 illustrates the decrease in scrap created by human error and the sustained improvement.

## New Device

Training produced zero-scrap goal achievement. Figure 7 shows how training achieved the zero-scrap goal and sustained that level of improvement.

## Novellus

Training produced a 65.9 percent decrease in scrap and a 260 percent ROI within five months. The goal for the Novellus Check-sheet Team was zero scrap. Figure 8 illustrates how the zero-scrap goal was achieved.

## Level 5

Return-on-investment ranged from 260 percent to 562 percent in the four implementation areas. Intangible goals met were improved employee morale, increased supervisor involvement, personal commitment to doing it right the first time, and personal pride.

## Communicating Results

The training scorecard gave a structured model for communicating comprehensive results on six levels. Level 0 was used by management

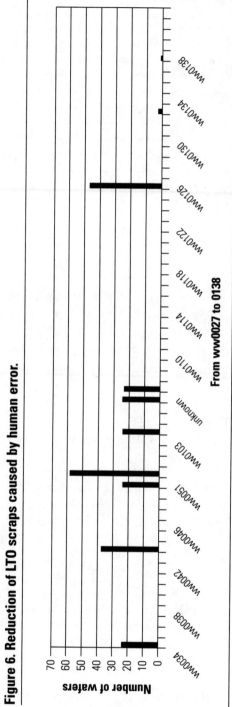

Figure 6. Reduction of LTO scraps caused by human error.

**Figure 7. A decrease to zero in new part scrap following training.**

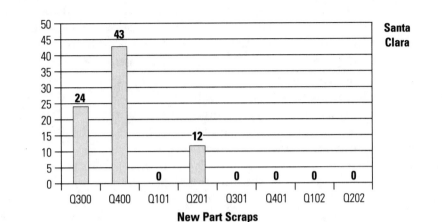

**Figure 8. Scrap per quarter reduced to zero.**

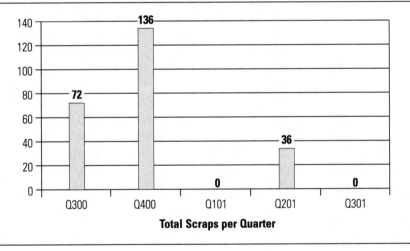

to identify strategic areas to target for cost reduction and to set metric improvement goals, which were communicated downward to the production-line level. Level 1 surveys were used to ensure that content and training were successfully received by trainees and to promote the positive training experiences for trainees—and that assisted in garnering further buy-in at the operator and supervisor levels.

Level 2 was used to communicate to the production supervisors what they could expect from people who had undergone the training. Level 3 was used to increase involvement of supervisors and enable them to communicate to line trainers and training coordinators their verification of on-the-job skill transfer and training results. Level 4 was the most effective tool used by management to communicate to the whole of the organization the impact of the training program and to recognize the participants and their achievements. Level 5 was used to show upper and middle management the efficacy of the investment in training during an economic downturn.

Communication of results using the training scorecard was done by the training coordinator. She was the project manager, the person most knowledgeable in the training system and the target areas, and she coordinated with management the work of all four teams. Her audience was the operators and their supervisors, whom she kept informed of the timeline, schedule, training process, and logistics. Her audience considered her very credible because of her knowledge and her 20 years of service with the company.

PowerPoint presentations were used to communicate to both management and shift supervisors. Email was used to schedule training classes and a quarterly report was produced as part of a detailed business report that went to management. Weekly staff meetings were used to update the teams on progress and timeline milestones. Bulletin boards similar to storyboards were used to show progress for companywide access and information exchange.

Managers were interested in detailed financial information. Operators were interested in who had undergone training and who was lined up for the training program. Because results were meeting expectations, no negative data emerged and none was communicated.

## Lessons Learned
- A six-level training scorecard is a powerful enabler to correlate training and its impact on metrics.
- A training scorecard forces training to be accountable for its results.
- Trainee feedback is essential to continuous improvement.
- Linking performance improvement to metric improvement further enhanced performance.
- Leadership commitment is critically important in driving training initiatives.
- Emphasis on quality increases productivity and raises employee morale.

- Specification/work procedure review, reassessment, revision, and testing are important to ensure quality and alignment to processes and comprehension by operators on the production line.
- One hundred percent proficiency can be attained with uniformity across the entire workforce.

## Questions for Discussion

1. What are the strengths and weaknesses of the strategies used to deploy the training scorecard to isolate the impact of training?
2. What would you have done differently to improve the application of this training scorecard?
3. Which elements of the training scorecard could be used to help managers improve supervisor accountability?
4. Why does conducting an effective Level 0 front-end analysis increase financial ROI?
5. How can you use this case study to improve the application of a training scorecard to your organization?

## The Authors

Mo Maghsoudnia is sponsor and operations/technology manager at ADI Santa Clara. He has a master's degree in electrical engineering, more than 15 years of experience in high-tech manufacturing, and 12 years with ADI specializing in process integration and development. As the manager over wafer fabrication operations, including process technology development and manufacturing/process engineering, equipment engineering, and production, Maghsoudnia has 10 direct and 150 indirect reports. He is responsible for wafer shipments generating revenue of $200 million per year and is a key member of the management team in charge of developing companywide business and operational strategies. He can be reached at 408.562.2604 or at mozafar.maghsoudnia@analog.com.

Lucy Strandberg is team leader and training manager at ADI. She has more than 30 years' experience in the semiconductor industry, with five of her 15 years at ADI spent as a training manager. She manages training initiatives at two wafer manufacturing sites and has 10 years' experience as a production manager, with seven shifts reporting to her. Her expertise in driving quality programs has helped her work successfully with multinational clients, such as Intel, IBM, and Motorola. She has led quality teams in achieving ISO 9000 certification and in meeting stringent military aeronautics requirements. Strandberg graduated from the University of Phoenix, with a business degree and a two-year background in semiconductor processing.

## References

Hubbard, L. Ron. (2002). *The Key to Effective Learning Lectures*. Santa Ana, CA: Effective Education Publishing.

Kirkpatrick, Donald L. (1998). *Evaluating Training Programs: The Four Levels*. 2nd ed. San Francisco: Berrett-Koehler.

Phillips, Jack J. (1997). *Handbook of Training Evaluation and Measurement Methods: Proven Models and Methods for Evaluating Any HRD Program*. 3rd ed. Boston: Butterworth-Heinemann.

# SQC Problem-Solving Training Program

## Toyota Industries Corporation

Uichi Tsutsumi and Susumu Kubota
Translated and edited by Kyoko Watanabe and Pat Patterson

*When top management at Toyota Industries Corporation (TICO) became aware that senior engineers were no longer showing the level of problem-solving talent expected of them, they decided to focus training on these engineers in hopes of strengthening statistical quality control (SQC) problem solving. Aware that training results are usually ambiguous and not well accepted by executives, the HRD-SQC group decided to use a scorecard for evaluation purposes. They knew that a scorecard offers clear results that executives can understand and accept, but the idea is still new in Japan. This would be a first, and it would offer a meaningful test of the hypothesis that improving competencies pays off for the organization. With assistance from JMA Management Center, Inc. (JMAM), Jack Phillips's scorecard was used to evaluate the program on Levels 1 through 4. TICO is now convinced of the value of scorecard evaluation and will continue to use it, thus setting an example that other Japanese companies are likely to follow.*

## The Company

Toyota Industries Corporation, with headquarters in Aichi prefecture in the center of Japan, is the parent company of Toyota Motor Corporation. Since its founding in 1926, TICO has expanded from the textile machinery sector into automobiles, engines, compressors, industrial vehicles, logistics systems, electronics, and casting. In fiscal 2001, its 22,877 employees generated a gross revenue of 980.2 billion yen.

Along with aggressive expansion into new business fields, TICO has worked constantly to enhance productivity and technology levels.

*This case was prepared to serve as a basis for discussion rather than to illustrate either effective or ineffective administrative and management practices.*

Its training programs have an excellent reputation in Japan and are emulated by other companies.

## The Challenge

In the last couple of years, TICO's top management became concerned about the level of their engineers' problem-solving skills. TICO's engineers were not performing at as high a level as those of some companies in the group, such as those at Toyota Motor Corporation. They did not show the same level of originality or creativity. TICO wanted to create high-performing engineers who would be esteemed as leaders, and management considered this an urgent challenge. They realized that engineers didn't use basic statistical quality control knowledge because the *kaizen* presentations by engineers incorporated few SQC ideas. *Kaizen* events are spoken of throughout this chapter. *Kaizen* is a broad label applied to any positive change in the workplace. A *kaizen* event is the achieving of some measurable or observable improvement, such as enhancing quality, lowering costs, shortening production cycles, simplifying delivery schemes, making common-sense improvements, or refining critical processes.

The SQC group had to solve this problem. Strengthening practical SQC was made a priority. For this training challenge, the company set a performance goal of reducing production costs by 30 percent with gross revenue at 1 trillion yen. At the same time, there needed to be an increase in contributions to the level of technology, as measured by the number of academic papers and outside presentations made by TICO engineers.

Since it put self-directed career development into practice in 1998 with the design of "Value Competencies," the company management had been noticing the importance of competencies. They theorized that not only skills and knowledge but also competencies contribute to company success. It was decided to include competencies as well as SQC skills in the problem-solving training program for engineers in order to test that theory.

Prior to this training program, TICO did not include competencies in any problem-solving training. SQC is a methodology based on fact and data, and the old style of training was based largely on lectures addressing practical knowledge and skills. That no longer seemed good enough.

In the new training program, individual feedback sessions and action plans were desirable in order to improve training effectiveness. The SQC group offers consulting services to individual engineers, so they have experience in giving feedback.

## Why the Use of a Scorecard Was Considered

TICO implemented a scorecard because the company wanted to know if participants contributed to business results and, if so, whether the contributions were a result of the training. Would participants achieve *kaizen* results attributable to the training? To find out, an action plan was designed as one tool for the scorecard.

The scorecard was intended not only for training evaluation but also motivating participants. Motivating growth is very important for training, and collecting before-and-after data gives good motivation as participants can be shown how much they have improved. Previously, the SQC group conducted Level 1 evaluation through a satisfaction questionnaire that contributed nothing to motivation, so a higher level of evaluation was needed.

Even though Level 1 evaluation is helpful, the SQC group needed more specific information in order to improve the quality of their training programs. The request for a scorecard did not come from company executives but from the SQC group itself, because they wanted to know that they contributed to TICO's business results.

## How the Implementation Occurred

In Japan only very technical fields have specialists. Most employees change departments every few years. In 1998 one of the authors (Susumu Kubota) was employed in the HRD department at TICO. With the assistance of consultants from JMAM, he set up for employees a self-directed career development program based on value competencies. After three years, the company was convinced of the importance of competencies because it seemed that the success shown in *kaizen* events was attributable not only to SQC proficiency but also to the competencies.

In 2000 Kubota was again put in charge of quality control training. He attended JMAM's annual HR conference when Jack Phillips was the keynote speaker and participated in Phillips's postconference workshop at JMAM. He was excited by the scorecard methodology presented and understood that a scorecard is very effective for measuring training and can be used to stimulate trainees' motivation. When his group was given the challenge to raise the SQC skills of senior engineers, Kubota saw an excellent opportunity to try the new methodology. His colleagues and supervisor supported the innovation, and top management approved a trial implementation.

When Kubota and his colleagues in the SQC group realized that problem-solving abilities are related to competencies, they realized how JMAM had supported value competencies through the first years and they thought JMAM was the right partner to help establish their new style of training. JMAM has a very good reputation in the competency field and is considered to be the best in training evaluation. Two years earlier, JMAM had carried out several cases of training evaluation to Level 3, and they were eager to have an opportunity to carry the process further, so their interests coincided with TICO's interests.

With internal approvals in place, Kubota approached Tsutsumi and his colleagues at JMAM to help with program design and evaluation. TICO had been a client of JMAM's for more than 20 years so they had worked together frequently. Furthermore, JMAM had translated and introduced to the Japanese market Phillips's *Handbook of Training Evaluation and Measurement Methods* (1997).

## Training Scorecard Methodology

Jack Phillips's (1997) model with Levels 1 through 4 was chosen for the training scorecard. Figure 1 shows the program design and scorecard TICO used for this course. What follows is a discussion of those levels in the TICO program.

### Level 1: Reaction

At the end of day one of the three-day program, a reaction questionnaire based on JMAM's standard format (table 1) was used to evaluate the day's program contents.

On the last day of the training session, TICO again used a reaction questionnaire to measure participants' satisfaction. Measurement was on the Likert Scale, with 1 representing strong disagreement and 5 indicating strong agreement. JMAM's format includes overall satisfaction plus seven factors that affect the rating, with each factor assessed in five to seven questions. TICO eliminated the environment factor and inserted an open-ended question soliciting suggestions for improving the program. Although response to that question required more time and effort, it was important in that first trial to gather participants' opinions and ideas for modifying the new approach to training.

The SQC group used Microsoft Excel software to determine the mean results and standard deviation and then further analyze the results.

### Level 2: Learning

Testing is the common way to measure learning. For program evaluation, TICO and JMAM usually design a test, conduct it on the last day of the program, and so measure the degree to which participants have acquired skills and knowledge from the training. But in this case

**Figure 1. Scorecard used for TICO's SQC problem-solving training program for senior engineers.**

| Level | Items for Evaluation | Methodology | Evaluator | Timing | Results |
|---|---|---|---|---|---|
| **1 Reaction** | Overall satisfaction<br>Understanding of content<br>Program design<br>Administration<br>Instructors/instruction<br>Materials<br>Ability to learn and later to apply content<br>Suggestions for improvement (open-ended) | Questionnaire (five-point scale) | Participants | Last day of training | Improve the program<br>Increase satisfaction |
| **2 Learning** | **Action plan:**<br>Level of challenge<br>Originality<br>Coherence of *kaizen* purpose, goal, and plan<br>Logical consistency<br>Foresight<br>Concreteness of results | Evaluating participants' action plans<br><br>Two-step assessment:<br>First: pass / fail<br>Then, if passed: excellent / good | Instructors and administration team | Submitted within one week after the end of the course | See if learning objectives were reached<br><br>Give feedback to participants<br><br>Give supervisors' support<br><br>Help participants set goals |
| **3 Application** | Competencies | Competency assessments (pre- and posttraining) (seven-point scale before, two-point scale after)<br><br>Compare before-and-after results | Pretraining: participants and supervisors<br><br>Posttraining: supervisors only | Before training and six months after training | Understand gains in competencies<br><br>Provide chances to develop competencies<br><br>OJT reference |
| **4 Business results** | *Kaizen* events<br>Monetary value of *kaizen* events (productivity, cost reductions, quality improvement, and so on) | Follow-up survey (open-ended)<br>Participants' estimates of monetary value of *kaizen* results | Participants | Six months after training | Improve the program<br>Increase program contributions to company success |

**Table 1. The eight factors in JMAM's standard reaction questionnaire.**

| Factor | Core Matter of Interest Underlying the Factors |
|---|---|
| Overall satisfaction | On the whole, are you satisfied with the training program? |
| Understanding of content | Did you understand the skills and knowledge presented as learning objectives? |
| Program design | Was the training program well designed for its desired results? |
| Administration | Was the session administered smoothly without causing you stress? |
| Instructors/instruction | Were the instructors effective? |
| Materials | Were the materials (texts, handouts, and audiovisual presentations) appropriate and helpful? |
| Ability to learn and later to apply content | Did you understand how to apply these lessons to your work? |
| Environment (classrooms) | Were the facilities appropriate, comfortable, and free of distractions? |

they did not use normal tests as Level 2 measurement tools because of two realizations made during their series of competency-identifying interviews of high performers:

1. High performers have a concrete image of their goal in mind before starting any problem-solving or *kaizen* activities.

2. High-performers envision obstacles they may encounter along the way to their goal, and plan ways to surmount such obstacles so they are prepared when difficulties arise.

If these two elements are essential to engineers' success in *kaizen* events, it would be necessary to evaluate participants' ability to conceptualize in those two ways. Having each participant design a personal action plan would best illustrate such ability. Participants were given one week after the end of the training session to make an action plan to help them achieve *kaizen* events on the job. The format of the action plan is shown in figure 2.

# Figure 2. TICO action plan format.

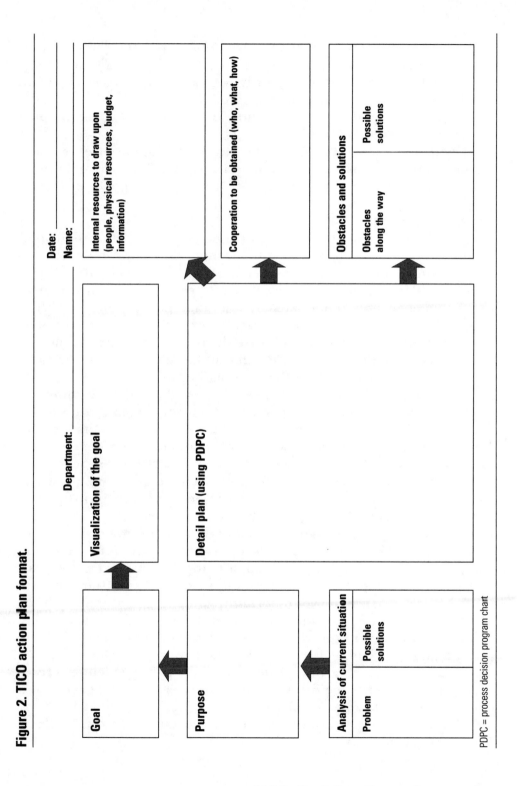

TICO instructors evaluated participants' action plans to see if they had appropriate content, defined concrete goals, had a valid theme, and showed an understanding of how to apply SQC knowledge and skills. Evaluation occurred in two steps:

1. A pass/fail judgment was made on whether the action plan reached the standard guideline for content.

2. Plans that passed the first review were rated good or excellent. Thus, there were three possible ratings for each action plan to illustrate the participants' understanding of SQC: excellent, good, or fail.

## Level 3: Application

*Step 1:* Data from the pretraining questionnaire, "Process Scope," completed by participants and their supervisors was evaluated. Its seven-point scale showed the degree to which participants already possessed the desired competencies. When Process Scope was distributed, the course pamphlet was attached so that participants and their supervisors would know what the learning objectives were. It was hoped that that information would increase the reliability of the evaluations and the completion ratio of the questionnaire, which was due to be turned in three days before the training began.

*Step 2:* Six months after the training session, with a deadline two days prior to presentations, supervisors again completed Process Scope questionnaires on participants' competencies. Comparing the pre- and posttraining sets of data showed the development of competencies.

TICO and JMAM discussed the two rounds of Process Scope and decided to change the rating scale in the 60-item questionnaires. The pretraining Process Scope used a seven-point scale. Given the subjective nature of such ratings and the likelihood that supervisors would not remember precisely how they had rated a participant six months earlier, it would be possible for a supervisor to give some posttraining competencies a lower score than before, even if the supervisor thought the competency had been improved. Because the team was much more concerned with determining improvement than with fixing a score for any one point in time, it decided that for each question in posttraining Process Scope, supervisors should simply indicate that a behavior had or had not been improved.

*Step 3:* The SQC group project members gave participants feedback, emphasizing the positive in order to illustrate their growth and to motivate higher performance.

*Step 4:* The SQC group prepared feedback reports in MSExcel for each participant.

The starting level of competencies was not at issue. TICO's concern throughout the program focused on developing competencies. Whatever the starting level, improvement was sought. The training scorecard was important not only for training evaluation, but also as a tool to motivate the program's participants in their work. The group was interested in giving participants opportunities to demonstrate their competencies and achieve *kaizen* events. TICO and JMAM had developed a value competencies dictionary for engineers three years earlier; at the outset of this program they prepared a competency dictionary specifically for the problem-solving abilities. JMAM drew on its broad experience to select the behaviors to include as competencies, and then the high-performing engineers' comments and explanations recorded in their interviews were incorporated verbatim. This was done because program designers and project members might not understand certain nuances and contexts the way a fellow engineer would; using unedited comments would make the competencies dictionary authentic and thereby more meaningful. At the *kaizen* event presentation six months after the training session, some participants offered gratifying feedback, saying that they read the competencies dictionary repeatedly and that consulting it showed them how to surmount obstacles.

## Level 4: Business Results

The final component of this program was a series of *kaizen* result presentations from the participants six months after the training days. Each participant presented a self-assessment of his or her business impact, evaluating *kaizen* events in the six-month interval and the improvements that could be traced to the program, such as productivity gains, cost reductions, quality improvements, and so on. The participant estimated the monetary value of these changes. The participants in the program were senior engineers, subsection chiefs, not in charge of an entire section but of a rank expected to contribute directly to performance levels. Their estimates of the contributions made by *kaizen* events and the monetary value of these contributions are significant to the organization and as reinforcement to the participants themselves. TICO wanted this performance evaluation process to prompt participants to view results from two perspectives: the contributions they had made to the organization, and the expectations the organization had of engineers in their position.

The *kaizen* presentation days were experiments. Believing that developing competencies is an important learning objective, the team wanted the presentations to be one more way to develop competencies.

A typical scenario would have participants show their performance and results in a cut-and-dried presentation. But in this program the SQC group wanted to examine the thoughts behind the actions. The participants were to answer probing questions: "Why did you choose your particular *kaizen* goal? Was there any one deciding factor in your choice? What obstacles did you encounter while trying to achieve your *kaizen* goal? How did you feel, and what did you think, when you encountered each obstacle? How did you overcome each obstacle?" Because the goal was to develop competencies, the process was more interesting than the results. The contexts of and reasons for participants' behavior needed to be understood. Also, participants should have opportunities to use their skills and knowledge. The process-based presentation event met two objectives:
1. to make participants more fully aware of their behavior patterns and offer an opportunity for self-examination
2. to help participants understand the reasoning processes of high performers.

Some participants were bewildered by the new style of presentation demanded of them. Nonetheless, the SQC group project members were convinced that participants would not be able to develop higher levels of competencies until they became sufficiently conscious of their current behavior patterns and reasoning to explain themselves to the group. Self-awareness is crucial to the development desired.

## Training Scorecard Application

The first step was to develop the competencies dictionary for senior engineers. High performers were selected and interviewed by the SQC project team. With JMAM's guidance, competencies were identified and extracted from the interview results. Next, the SQC project team clarified the work flow in the engineering department. A good understanding of the department then allowed the development of the competencies dictionary in an appropriate context. Finally, a questionnaire called "Process Scope" was designed as our tool to assess the competencies defined in the new dictionary. Table 2 gives an overview of the course plan, evaluation tools, and evaluation levels.

The training program was designed around competencies and practical SQC skills. Tools for the program, such as assessment sheets and feedback forms, were created. Two examples are offered here. Figure 3, the competencies development plan, shows how competency

**Table 2. SQC problem-solving training course comprehensive design steps.**

| | Phase 1 | Phase 2 | Phase 3 | Phase 4 |
|---|---|---|---|---|
| **Objectives** | Designing and assessing the program | Delivering the program | Providing opportunities to use learned skills | Grasping training's contribution to business results |
| **Action items** | Designing the program<br>Making a competency model<br>Measuring participants' competencies | Conducting the problem-solving competencies training program<br>Conducting the practical SQC skills training program | Applying SQC skills to real work situation through *kaizen* events<br>Providing chances to develop competencies through *kaizen* events | Presenting *kaizen* results<br>Converting *kaizen* results to monetary value<br>Understanding gains in competencies<br>Identifying training program effects on business results |
| **Training evaluation tools** | Level: | 1. *Reaction questionnaire:* Checks participants' satisfaction with the program and suggests future modifications.<br>2. *Action plan sheet:* Shows if they are ready to carry out *kaizen* action plan and if they know what kind of cooperation should be gained.<br>3. *Process scope:* 360-degree assessment too: reveals gains in competencies.<br>4. *Kaizen results sheet for presentation day:* Shows monetary value of *kaizen* results and the program's contributions to company success. | | |
| **Timeline** | Level 4: Design index to measure business results<br><br>Level 3: Find current level of competencies | Conduct training program Level 2:<br>Specify which competencies should be developed<br>Understand *kaizen* action plan Level 1:<br>Find the degree of participants' satisfaction with the training program | | Level 4: Confirm monetary value of improved business results<br><br>Level 3: Discover gains in competencies |

goals were put in focus, with a target behavior and a plan for achieving each goal. Figure 4 presents a self-assessment tool, "Your Work Style,"
used to help participants raise their self-awareness and reflect on the
degree to which they had demonstrated the desired competencies.

Finally, the training scorecard assessment tools were decided
upon: Level 1, the reaction questionnaire; Level 2, the action plans
(see figure 2); Level 3, Process Scope, a form of 360-degree feedback;
and Level 4, the self-assessment of participants' contributions to the
company, in monetary terms.

Figure 5 depicts JMAM's Level 4 self-assessment sheet for an individual's contribution to company success. It served as the basis for
TICO's questionnaire, although it is not the exact one used.

This training program for senior engineers ran three full days,
with a half-day follow-up session six months later. There were 124 participants, divided into four groups—first two groups totaling 70 engineers and then two groups totaling 54.

We used a Process Scope pretraining assessment in which participants
and their supervisors rated the degree to which the participants demonstrated desired competencies on the job. The supervisors completed
an additional questionnaire detailing the roles they expected each
participant to play in the organization and the kinds of on-the-job
behavior they wished to see.

## Curriculum, Day One: SQC and Competencies

"SQC = problem solving" was the company's message to engineers.
TICO does not think of SQC as limited to statistical quality control,
but rather as an umbrella term for all problem-solving initiatives. Instructors began by explaining that the company wants and expects
engineers to use many methodologies.

Next, instructors presented the competencies of high performers and how they had been extracted from interviews.

Last, the SQC group gave participants feedback from Process Scope,
the pretraining assessment of their competencies. Trainees became
aware of differences between their supervisors' perceptions and their
own self-assessments. With an understanding of their strong and weak
points, participants could plan how to develop competencies.

## Curriculum, Day Two: Applying SQC Skills in a Business Simulation

We designed a strategic engineering simulation posing five problems, three for this day and two for the following. Through lectures,
team discussion, modeling games, and group presentations addressing

# Figure 3. TICO competencies development plan.

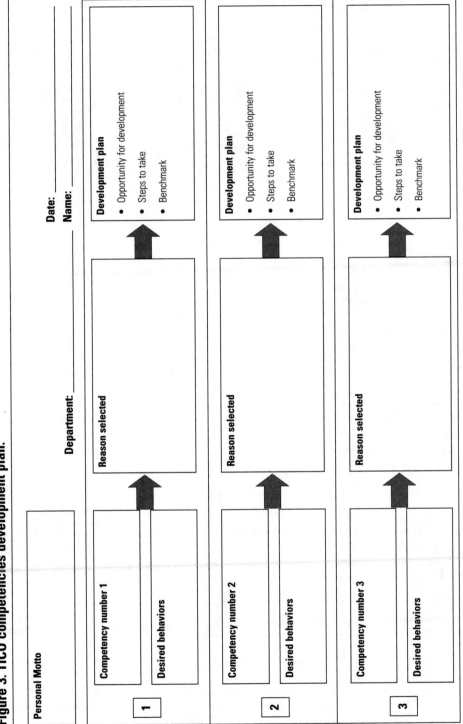

Personal Motto

Department: _____

Date: _____
Name: _____

**1**

**Competency number 1**

**Desired behaviors**

**Reason selected**

**Development plan**
- Opportunity for development
- Steps to take
- Benchmark

**2**

**Competency number 2**

**Desired behaviors**

**Reason selected**

**Development plan**
- Opportunity for development
- Steps to take
- Benchmark

**3**

**Competency number 3**

**Desired behaviors**

**Reason selected**

**Development plan**
- Opportunity for development
- Steps to take
- Benchmark

## Figure 4. Your work style.

Date _____

Department _____

Name _____

Please choose one current work theme or objective and enter it in the box at the top of the right-hand column. Then describe your behavior concretely, based on the competencies listed in the left-hand column.

| Your Work Theme or Objective | |
| --- | --- |
| Competencies | Behavior |
| Embracing assignments | |
| Getting to the heart of the matter | |
| Taking a multifaceted perspective | |
| Seeking and mastering information | |
| Coping quickly and flexibly | |
| Sticking to a goal | |
| Thinking ahead | |
| Reaching out for cooperation | |
| Using knowledge and information effectively | |
| Demonstrating a professional engineering mentality | |

each problem, participants could experience typical applications of SQC methodologies. The simulation involved the design and production of a spring-driven, resinous toy car called "Toyo Q." The SQC group had technical books and toy cars at the ready to inspire and support problem-solving during team discussions.

*Problem one: coming up with an overall plan to develop a new product.* The Process Decision Program Chart method was used.

*Problem two: preventing problems and failures.* The Failure Mode and Effects Analysis method was used.

*Problem three: investigating mechanisms and determining optimal operation.* The cross-experiment method was used, along with an experimental planning method game.

# Figure 5. Business impact questionnaire.

A. What was your *kaizen* theme this time?

B. Which category was your *kaizen* event in?

   1. ___ productivity
   2. ___ quality
   3. ___ cost reduction
   4. ___ production time
   5. ___ safety
   6. ___ morale
   ?     other (specify) _____

C. Choose up to five items that were enhanced as a result of this training:

   1. ___ ability to cope with problems
   2. ___ speed in solving problems
   3. ___ ability to stick with a project or problem to completion
   4. ___ communication within the project team
   5. ___ networking outside my team
   6. ___ communication with SQC team
   7. ___ better understanding of SQC
   8. ___ focus on target competencies
   9. ___ ability to make use of SQC Park (intranet)

D. Please use the following scale to answer this section:
   1 = almost never, 2 = seldom, 3 = occasionally, 4 = frequently, 5 = almost always

   1. While working toward *kaizen* goals, did you
     • use knowledge and skills learned from the training for actual *kaizen* events? _____
     • reread training materials? _____
     • access SQC Park? _____

   2. Thinking of organizational support, did you have
     • your supervisor's support and advice for *kaizen* events? _____
     • regular meetings with the supervisor about process management? _____
     • the cooperation of peers and subordinates? _____
     • the environment and all tools needed for *kaizen* activities? _____
     • help from or opportunities to consult the SQC group? _____

E. Please estimate the monetary value of the *kaizen* events you achieved. _____

F. How confident are you of that estimate? _____
   (0 percent = no confidence, 100 percent = completely convinced)

G. Please indicate the percent of your improvements or accomplishments that you consider directly related to the training program, and then explain your estimate. _____
   (0 percent = no contribution, 100 percent = full contribution)

### Curriculum, Day Three: Finishing up the Simulation and Beginning Action Plans

*Problem four: deciding design dimensions.* Quality engineering parameter design was used.

*Problem five: avoiding bad quality in the production line.* Multiple regression analysis and principal component analysis were used, along with a multivariate analysis method game.

When the simulation was completed, instruction was given for preparing an individual action plan to achieve a *kaizen* event on the job. Participants had one week to complete their plans, but they got under way with guidance from the SQC group.

### Follow-through, Six Months Later: Preparing for the Presentations

Supervisors were asked to observe and evaluate the training participants on the job in this interval and then to complete a Process Scope questionnaire similar to the pretraining assessment. When the SQC group invited participants to make their presentations, they attached a Level 4 assessment sheet that participants were required to complete and bring with them. It evaluated the effect of their training and assessing their own impact on business results, putting a monetary value on their contribution. The SQC group instructed participants on the kind of presentation they should make and the handouts they should prepare to support their presentations.

### Follow-through: The Presentations and Feedback

Each participant had 20 minutes to present *kaizen* process(es) and results, followed by 10 minutes of questions and answers. The SQC group asked about any secrets of success, special techniques, and the details of problem-solving processes used.

Six presentations were scheduled for each half-day session. Participants attended only the session of their own presentation. Hearing five colleagues provided a reasonable sample of the range of presentations without interrupting work for long periods of time and without risk of boredom from a repetitive format.

After the presentations, the SQC group asked participants to reread and reflect upon their Level 4 business impact evaluations before submitting them. No changes were being made; it was simply to have participants reflect on the value of what they had done.

The final component of the program involved feedback from the SQC group on the posttraining Process Scope evaluation by the supervisors. Participants were encouraged to speak directly with their supervisors after the feedback sessions. The SQC Group also reported their assessments of the contributions the training and subsequent *kaizen* events had made to business results.

## Training Evaluation Results

Figure 6 shows the scorecard with summary results. Let's take each level in turn.

### Level 1 Evaluation: Reaction, Measured on Questionnaires

Table 3 presents the ratings the two training groups gave to the program.

- *What Participants Reported.* Participants did not report high satisfaction with the course. One reason was the team's failure adequately to communicate the purpose of the training and its relative importance to TICO. Participants did not understand the relationship between developing competencies and achieving *kaizen* events at work. Participants also were not satisfied with the training design and administration for day one, when participants had to transcribe data from their individual Process Scope report into another sheet and consolidate their opinions on that sheet. It took longer than expected so they did not have enough time to reflect on their supervisors' evaluations and then to consolidate their opinions. There also was insufficient time for group discussion of methods and opportunities to develop competencies. Low satisfaction further stemmed from a little negative feeling about the supervisors' ratings of their competencies. Not yet having had any chance to discuss the ratings, participants could feel that supervisors might not know them and their work well enough for the ratings to be fair and accurate.

- *What Was Observed.* During the simulation exercises on days two and three, the team realized that most participants lacked the knowledge of SQC methodology that the program designers had expected. They had had basic SQC training, but had not applied its techniques on the job and so had lost the knowledge without ever having understood its possible applications. That limited their understanding of the program and hindered their ability to grasp its lessons on how to apply SQC methods in their work.

The participants did not like the simulation exercises having so little resemblance to their current work, and did not manage to extract principles and processes they could use.

**Figure 6. Scorecard results.**

| Level | Items for Evaluation | Methodology | Evaluator | Timing | Results |
|-------|---------------------|-------------|-----------|--------|---------|
| **1**<br>**Reaction** | Overall satisfaction<br>Understanding of content<br>Program design<br>Administration<br>Instructors/instruction<br>Materials<br>Ability to learn and later to apply content<br>Suggestions for improvement (open-ended) | Questionnaire (five-point scale) | Participants | Last day of training | Satisfaction ratings (five-point scale):<br>First group: 3.32<br>Second group: 3.28 |
| **2**<br>**Learning** | **Action plan:**<br>Level of challenge<br>Originality<br>Coherence of *kaizen* purpose, goal, and plan<br>Logical consistency<br>Foresight<br>Concreteness of results | Evaluating participants' action plans<br><br>Two-step assessment:<br>First: pass / fail<br>Then, if passed: excellent / good | Instructors and administration team | Submitted within one week after the end of the course | 114 passed, 9 failed |
| **3**<br>**Application** | Competencies | Competency assessments (pre- and posttraining) (seven-point scale before, two-point scale after)<br><br>Compare before-and-after results | Pretraining: participants and supervisors<br><br>Posttraining: supervisors only | Before training and six months after training | Top three gains in competencies:<br><br>Understands own role in company goals<br><br>Takes on assignments willingly and proactively<br><br>Deals with problems one by one proactively, no matter how many there are |
| **4**<br>**Business results** | *Kaizen* events<br>Monetary value of *kaizen* events (productivity, cost reductions, quality improvement, and so on) | Follow-up survey (open-ended)<br>Participants' estimates of monetary value of *kaizen* results | Participants | Six months after training | More than 40 million yen |

**Table 3. Level 1 mean results on a five-point Likert scale.***

|  | First Two Teams | Last Two Teams |
|---|---|---|
| Overall rating | 3.32 | 3.28 |
| Understanding of the content | 4.04 | 4.01 |
| Program design | 3.55 | 3.67 |
| Administration | 3.96 | 4.00 |
| Instructors/instruction | 3.76 | 3.81 |
| Materials | 3.53 | 3.54 |
| Ability to learn and later to apply content | 3.35 | 3.31 |

*5 = strongly agree.

They also were locked in an engineering mentality of expecting a "right" answer to every problem, and were unhappy with the instructors' attempts to guide them to apply their own solutions, without ever indicating "right" or "wrong." This reaction revealed the dichotomy between what their jobs require and what their training had taught. The gap was a defect of basic SQC training.

The participants were able to solve the simulation problems through group discussion and teamwork but did not come away feeling confident that they could apply the methodologies on their own back at their jobs. They wanted to be told *exactly* how to apply the training lessons to their daily work.

Training design can be blamed for some of the dissatisfaction. The timing of the program was another problem because the course was held during a period of interviews for promotion when participants were distracted by anxiety over their futures.

### Level 2 Evaluation: Learning, Demonstrated in Action Plans

Although the participants were not very satisfied with the training program, 114 of them completed satisfactory action plans. Table 4 shows what was considered in evaluating the action plans, and table 5 presents the results of the Level 2 evaluation.

## Table 4. Evaluation items and points for an action plan.

| Number | Items for Evaluation | Evaluation Points |
|---|---|---|
| 1 | *Kaizen* theme | Level of challenge, originality, innovation |
| 2 | Image of *kaizen* results | Clarity and concreteness of image of goal |
| 3 | Coherence of *kaizen* purpose, goal, and plan | Coherence of *kaizen* purpose, goal, and plan<br>Logic shown in *kaizen* purpose, goal, and plan |
| 4 | Prediction of obstacles and solutions | Foresight shown in solutions offered to anticipated obstacles<br>Concreteness of solutions |

## Table 5. Level 2 evaluation results.

| Step One | Step Two | Number of Participants* |
|---|---|---|
| Pass | Excellent | 35 |
| | Good | 79 |
| Fail | No further judgment | 9 |

*One participant did not complete an action plan, so the total here is 123 rather than 124.

## Level 3 Evaluation: Application, Measured by Process Scope Questionnaires

Many supervisors indicated that a majority of the target competencies were demonstrated more frequently than they had been prior to the training. Table 6 reports the target behaviors in which at least 60 percent of the participants showed improvement.

## Level 4 Evaluation: Business Results, Measured by Participants

Detailed contribution data is confidential but some information can be shared. The goal of reducing production costs by 30 percent was not achieved, but the SQC problem-solving training course provided *kaizen* results with a monetary value to TICO of more than 40 million yen.

**Table 6. Level 3 evaluation results: behavior reported as improved for at least 60 percent of participants.**

| Behaviors | Percent of Participants Who Improved |
|---|---|
| Takes on assigned work willingly and proactively | 83.9 |
| Understands own role in reaching company goals | 96.4 |
| When a problem occurs, tries to understand not only what is happening, but also why | 71.4 |
| Makes sure he or she has understood an assignment | 67.3 |
| Thinks not only from an engineer's point of view, but also from that of the end user | 62.3 |
| Listens carefully to others' advice, even if he or she disagrees | 63.9 |
| Deals with problems one by one proactively, no matter how many there are | 77.0 |
| Facing apparently insurmountable obstacle, he or she still believes a solution can be found and tries to move forward | 67.2 |
| When a problem cannot be solved within his or her own group or division, tries cooperating with other groups | 73.8 |
| Analyzes data from a theoretical view and seeks new knowledge | 60.7 |
| Remains on the lookout for unexpected problems | 65.6 |

Here are some of the participants' comments about the intangible effects of the training:

- It was useful and informative to have to present my work and get to listen to others' presentations. That helped me take another look at my own job and think about how I should work from now on.
- I could understand what role my supervisor expects of me, and so determine an appropriate goal.
- Preparation of the presentation six months after the training was very hard and honestly it was a troublesome job. However, others' presentations gave me ideas about the tough issues and obstacles they had faced and what their background was. That was very useful information.

- I could learn which situations call for which methodologies.
- I could get good ideas of how to plan a project from start to finish when I was given the challenge, "Developing a New Product."

## Communicating Results

JMAM reported its scorecard measurements, including the collected data and its analysis and summary report, to TICO's training administration team, the HRD-SQC group. The SQC group made its own scorecard following the same process but with some internal reports of its own, and presented it to the executive in charge of training initiatives. The final scorecard was reported to top management.

### Level 1 Report

Two weeks after the training sessions, the SQC group made a summary report and an oral presentation on the sessions to the director in charge of the training division. The group also reported to the senior executive in charge of training during the weekly training division meeting. Although the report covered the objectives and curriculum, it was concerned chiefly with Level 1 questionnaire results and suggestions for modifying the training. The SQC group submitted JMAM's report unaltered to the director.

### Levels 2 to 4

The SQC group had intensive internal discussions of the program and possible future modifications. There were no reports to individual executives. The group also met with Uichi Tsutsumi of JMAM to discuss Level 2-4 results and solicit advice for future programs. The SQC group then made a consolidated report delivered in an oral presentation to the director.

## Lessons Learned
- When an evaluation of the training process is planned from the outset, the training goals are clearer and more concrete than when evaluation is not part of the picture.
- Before a course begins, it is essential to let participants understand just what the learning objectives are and what kind of posttraining performance is expected of them.
- Participants must know they will have opportunities to demonstrate their learning. The follow-up after six months, with participants having to show what they have learned and get feedback on their performance, is essential to every future training program.

- It is very helpful to have an image of what maximum training success would be before beginning a program, just as the high performers create an image of complete success before starting a new project.
- It is important for Japanese managers in charge of training initiatives to realize the difference a scorecard makes. Too few Japanese companies have an appropriate index or sufficient data for measuring the business impact of training. The challenge now is to set criteria, build databases, and find ways to calculate the monetary value through Level 4.
- All in all, the SQC group is very satisfied that they created not only a new style of course for engineers and superior reports for management, but also a development system. TICO executives were very pleased that the scorecard gave a clear picture of the program's effectiveness.
- This type of scorecard will continue to be used because it is effective and motivating. In the near term, however, scorecards will be used only in the SQC group. Susumu Kubota understood the idea because of his background in statistics and his participation in Jack Phillips's workshop at JMAM's conference, but other training teams do not yet know this method of training evaluation, and so have no commitment to scorecard implementation. They need to *understand* it, not merely be required to apply it.

## Discussion Questions

1. What are the advantages and disadvantages of using action plans in place of normal testing to evaluate training effectiveness?
2. How could using training scorecard methodology change the design of training programs?
3. Do you think TICO's strategy to develop competencies was a good approach?
4. Why does TICO's SQC group now think that the implementation of a training scorecard methodology is essential?

## The Contributors

TICO's SQC group, a team in the training division of the HRD department created to further SQC methods in the TQM initiative in the company, implemented this SQC problem-solving training course. The five members of the SQC group are Toshio Kaneoka, Susumu Kubota, Hiroshi Mori, Hiroyuki Oiwa, and Shiho Saito. The group thinks in broader terms of problem solving than their name indicates.

They conduct training sessions for administrators as well as engineers. Their mission is to contribute to society and the organization through problem-solving perspectives that affect professional growth.

## The Authors and Translators/Editors

Uichi Tsutsumi is an evaluation professional at JMA Management Center Inc., which provides human resources management (HRM) and development solutions. (Its parent is Japan Management Association, a not-for-profit organization leading in HRM fields since 1942.) As an account executive for training services, Tsutsumi gained wide experience in designing, developing, and promoting correspondence education courses and assessment tools. Since 1999 he has been a project leader for training effectiveness research and has been actively disseminating the concept of training effectiveness in the Japanese market. Tsutsumi and Kyoko Watanabe interviewed U.S. companies for a special edition of *Jinzai-Kyouiku*, JMAM's HRM and HRD magazine, titled "Training Effectiveness in the U.S.," for which Tsutsumi served as chief editor. He can be reached at Uichi_Tsutsumi@jmam.co.jp.

Susumu Kubota joined TICO in 1987. For six years he was in charge of quality control training, and then joined an automobile system project. In 1997, Kubota was assigned to the HRD department, where he implemented the concept of competencies and created a career development system. Since 2000 he has again been in charge of quality control training and consulting on problem solving. In 2000 he encountered Jack Phillips's ideas about training evaluation and began planning the use of training scorecards to provide a much higher quality of training programs.

Kyoko Watanabe is a researcher and writer in the HRM field. She has worked with JMAM since 1988. While living in New York City for the last eight years, she has been an international coordinator for many research and investment projects.

Pat Patterson is a writer, editor, and language teacher who consults to professionals in many fields.

## Reference

Phillips, Jack J. (1997). *Handbook of Training Evaluation and Measurement Methods: Proven Models and Methods for Evaluating Any HRD Program.* 3rd ed. Boston: Butterworth-Heinemann.

# The Competitive Weapon: Using ROI Measurement to Drive Results

## Large-Tech Corporation

Theresa L. Seagraves

*This case study describes how an organization can change, drive, and optimize its return-on-investment (ROI) from performance improvement programs. This training scorecard illustrates how to connect ROI goals for a training program to executives' business strategy and how to use measurement to provide managers with data early and often enough that they can increase the impact of a training program before the final ROI calculations are complete. The study describes the methodology and how it has been used with a specialized sales group within a North American Fortune 500 technology company.*

## Critical Business Issue

Large-Tech offers a suite of high-technology hardware and software products to its customers. One product has emerged as a strategic part of its total offerings. Because the market for this product is in a hyper-growth state, the top two companies in this market will enjoy high profit margins, a large customer base, and long-term sales relationships. The top competitors will be able to leverage their relationships to sell other products to these customers. Large-Tech does not currently hold one of the top two positions in this market, although Large-Tech's product is as good as or superior to that of its competitors.

As this study began, senior management believed that Large-Tech had a one-year window during which it would either earn one of those

*This case was prepared to serve as a basis for discussion rather than to illustrate either effective or ineffective administrative and management practices. Names of places, organizations, or people have been disguised at the request of the author or organization. The sales situation and graphs have been altered to display similar but fictitious data. All of the key ratios and percentages have been maintained.*

two top positions or find itself in a long-term second-tier position. The former of those two options was a key business initiative.

## Performance Requirements

Large-Tech's salesforce was accustomed to selling at a low to middle level within their customers' organizations. Their conversations focused on product features, benefits, and price comparisons. Selling based on features, benefits, and price encourages buyers to view a product as a commodity, and it is difficult to convince a buyer that one commodity product is very different and worth a higher price than another. Large-Tech's new sales strategy targeted the top-level of customer organizations, the "C" level. "C" refers to the chief executive officer (CEO), chief financial officer (CFO), chief information officer (CIO), chief operating officer (COO), and similar positions. Large-Tech's salespeople needed to persuade the "C" level that Large-Tech's solution would help their long-term business strategies and improve their key financial metrics as return on assets, gross profit margin, and the cost of capital.

## Training Intervention

The training intervention was a course on financial selling. Led by former CFOs, the course taught Large-Tech's salespeople how to read balance sheets, income statements, U.S. Securities and Exchange Commission 10K and 10Q filings, and other financial documents, and how to identify fundamental business issues reflected in those reports. They learned how to position Large-Tech's solution to address those issues. By putting their salespeople through this training program, Large-Tech asked their salesforce to learn and successfully implement a very different and complex type of sale.

## State of the Intervention before the Scorecard

About half of Large-Tech's salesforce had taken a financial selling course in the previous year. Senior managers believed that their investment in this course would achieve great results, but very few of the participants implemented the methods taught. The training department could identify a few salespeople who had achieved dramatic results applying the methods taught in the course, and they believed the program had generated a positive ROI, but sales managers were not convinced.

The training department offered to perform an industry standard ROI study but the senior sales managers were not interested. It takes six months to close the average sale for this product, and sales managers believed that by the time they got an answer on whether the training was paying off, they either would have succeeded in their market or they would have failed and so be out of their jobs. The managers didn't want merely to measure ROI; they wanted to set ROI goals, monitor their progress, and drive the ROI as high as possible as quickly as they could.

## Training Scorecard Methodology

To address the sales managers needs, Large-Tech combined The Bottom Line ROI measurement system with its balanced scorecard initiative. The Bottom Line ROI (BLROI) is a U.S. patent-pending process developed to address many of the issues that Large-Tech faced. Kaplan and Norton introduced scorecards in their book *The Balanced Scorecard* (1996).

The BLROI process gathers a series of "snapshots," or estimates, of a participant's probable and actual behavior over time. To help the senior managers drive their ROI, the BLROI process graphed and summarized

- estimates of how quickly participants believed they would implement (their learning curve)
- rates of adoption
- ROI patterns
- benefit contributions from performance objectives promised by the vendor
- estimated and actual start of payback activity.

Using the scorecard and the graphs from the BLROI process, Large-Tech managers could understand their progress in 30 seconds or less. This gave them the opportunity to change their actions between each snapshot and improve their overall final return.

In addition to the quantitative data gathered to produce these metrics, the BLROI process also gathered qualitative data. The training department wanted to copy the best practices of top performers and teach them to others. They also wanted to know the key issues that needed to be addressed so that learning and performance could improve more quickly. Large-Tech's training department and sales managers received detailed reports and summaries of best practices and key issues that should be duplicated or addressed.

To understand the methodology used in this case study, it is important to tie together in a new way the concepts of business goal setting, learning curves, and training adoption. The BLROI process asks participants to estimate the *probability* that they will take a desired action and then it tracks their behavior, best practices, and key issues as they move from expectations to actual performance. The following sections outline the concepts of goal setting, learning curves, adoption models, and BLROI processes and graphs as a foundation for applying them to the training scorecard.

## Goal Setting and The Balanced Scorecard

Kaplan and Norton's balanced scorecard (BSC) expands the classic financial and customer satisfaction measurement processes into a method for managing the implementation of business strategy throughout an organization. The unique contribution of the BSC is the use of metrics from four perspectives: financial, customer, process, and learning and innovation.

The first step in the BLROI process is to connect the appropriate metrics in the BSC to a minimum ROI goal necessary from a training program. Because the BLROI methodology uses graphs and charts to communicate status quickly, setting a minimum ROI goal is necessary to know if the graphs are describing good news or bad.

To set this goal, the training department and management must work together to estimate four key pieces of information:

- cost of the training program and BLROI study.
- minimum, or *net,* revenue or savings benefit that must be gained from the training.
- estimated average percentage of credit that participants or other experts will attribute to the training program for improving revenue or savings. This is also known as the average *isolation factor.*
- actual, or *gross,* revenue or savings benefit that must be generated from the business to achieve the isolated, or net, benefit of the training.

Using the formula ([net benefit − costs]/costs) × 100 = ROI%, these numbers are converted into a percentage ROI goal for the training program. Dividing the net benefit by the estimated isolation factor yields the gross benefit that must be obtained from the business overall.

The expected gross benefit will be used to interpret graphs of business activity. The net benefit will be used to interpret benefit charts and graphs. The cost estimates and ROI target will be used to track breakeven time and gauge the rate of progress toward the ROI goal.

## Learning Curves

After setting ROI goals, the next step is to chart progress in meeting them. The first way is to plot a line demonstrating how quickly people *believe* they will implement new behaviors. Such lines are known as "learning curves." There are two common, but different, views of learning curves.

The first view of a learning curve, as shown in figure 1, is a "surface view." Represented by the straight line in figure 1, this view holds that following training, the participants should be able to implement skills and knowledge taught in a straightforward manner back on the job. It is assumed that ROI will be achieved at the tip of the arrow. For straightforward training programs that focus on relatively low levels of knowledge or for high-performing individuals who are capable of rapidly assimilating complex new skills, this curve may reflect reality.

For most people, however, the bigger or more discontinuous the change they are being asked to make, the more their learning curve resembles a logarithmic function (shown in figure 1 as the middle curve). In this view, initial on-the-job performance is often flat at best, and frequently dips below precourse levels, as participants struggle to change habits, use new language or skills, and become comfortable with altered performance expectations.

Adopting new behaviors on the job requires a period of adjustment. If the adjustment seems too difficult, transfer to the job never occurs and a participant's learning curve stays flat. Sooner or later, however,

**Figure 1. Two views of a learning curve.**

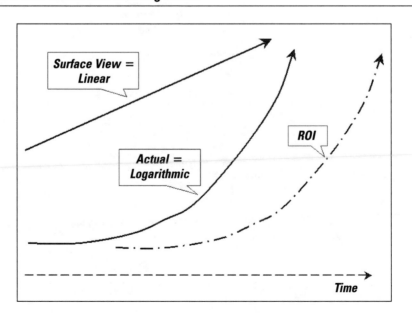

the successful participants will feel as though they have mastered the individual pieces. Their performance will begin to climb as they become confident and comfortable. As shown in figure 1, the ROI for their new performance will lag in time after the behavior change itself.

Graphs presented later in this case study will show how and when to look for both types of learning curves.

### Behavior Adoption, Change Management, and Performance Acceleration

Those learning curves can be overlaid on a model that helps managers track behavior adoption, manage change, and accelerate performance. This behavior adoption model, shown in figure 2, is based on a market model of new technology adoption made popular by Geoffrey Moore in his groundbreaking books, *Inside the Tornado* (1995) and *Crossing the Chasm* (1999). What follows is an explanation of the elements in and the concepts underlying this figure.

- *ROI Potential.* The first three items to observe in figure 2 are the bell curve, the course, and the ROI goal. Taken together, these represent

**Figure 2. Behavior adoption and ROI.**

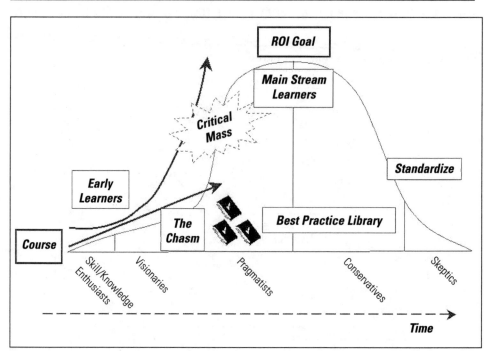

Adapted from *Inside the Tornado*, Geoffrey A. Moore, Copyright 1995, HarperCollins, New York, NY.

the optimum ROI for a group of participants in a course. The area under the curve of the bell represents the potential ROI. Every course starts at the entrance to the bell curve or at the entrance to its ROI potential. The ROI goal is set at the top of the bell. The left side of the bell curve shows increasing ROI. Following the bell down the right side shows diminishing returns from the additional time and effort required to gain the return.

- *Participant Types and Time to Adopt.* Next, observe in figure 2 the five types of participants spread over an arrow representing time. These participants are skill/knowledge enthusiasts, visionaries, pragmatists, conservatives, and skeptics. Over time, the skill/knowledge enthusiasts will be the first to adopt any new behavior; the skeptics will be last.

  Skill/knowledge enthusiasts are tactical contributors. Their value is in helping to ensure that a new training program is well designed with coherent concepts that are defined clearly and applied consistently within the program. Visionaries are strategic thinkers. They do not have to have a perfect solution before they will commit to a large, discontinuous change. They see so much value in what they have just learned that they will make the effort to fill in incomplete processes and will figure out how to make the performance leap back on the job. Pragmatists are the opposite of visionaries. Before they will adopt a large, discontinuous change, they want it to be as easy as possible and they want to be able to implement it in as little time as possible. They want to see that others have successfully used a process before implementing it themselves. Conservatives want everything the pragmatists want, plus special modifications to fit their personal situations. Finally, skeptics are the people who resist change so steadfastly that they will change only when faced with potential sanctions or given absolute guarantees that everything will go well.

- *The Chasm.* The next four items to examine in figure 2 are labeled "The Chasm," "Early Learners," "Main Stream Learners," and "Standardize." The chasm traps many promising training and performance improvement programs that never recover to deliver their potential. It is defined as the gap between the adoption of new behavior by early learners (skill/knowledge enthusiasts and visionaries) and the adoption of that same behavior by mainstream learners (pragmatists, conservatives, and skeptics).

  Understanding the pragmatist emphasis on using proven behavior with few issues is key to unlocking a large portion of the potential ROI. The chasm is crossed by demonstrating best practices, sharing success stories, and removing obstacles. Ideally, the early learners will complete a course first so that their best practices can be leveraged and copied by the pragmatists and so that any issues they raise can be removed quickly. This benefits the scorecard by making it easier for an organization to maintain and build momentum as it tracks ROI.

After reaching the target adoption level and ROI goal, an organization can move from managing change to standardizing the new level of behavior. Standardization occurs when the organization updates the training program, rewrites job performance expectations, and makes such other changes as updating marketing programs, IT systems, or other processes to reflect the change to a new standard of behavior.

- *Learning Curves, Best Practices, and Critical Mass.* Finally, take a look at the best practice library, critical mass, and the learning curves depicted to the left of the bell in figure 2. You can see why the surface view of learning occurs. Line managers often observe the early learners as they begin to apply new learning on the job. Based on what they see in the early learners, managers assume that the behavior of other types of learners will follow the same trajectory.

In reality, mainstream learners frequently *do not* follow the early learners without getting help crossing the chasm. The mainstream learners will follow the early learners slowly at first, depending on their match to the best practices that are built up and shared. Mainstream learners will follow more and more quickly as more best practices are made available and issues are removed. Critical mass, defined as the mass movement of a group of people to a new behavior, occurs rapidly when enough best practices have been shared to create strong proof of success and when those best practices are shared with the right levels of reward and reinforcement. At this point standardization can take place.

## ROI Measurement

The Bottom Line ROI is based on Jack J. Phillips's (1997) groundbreaking work on ROI measurement. Because this methodology draws pictures from repeatedly refined data sets, it is very important to follow a consistent, conservative, validated process each time data is collected.

The BLROI uses a repeated series of estimates from course participants to draw graphs and charts of behavior and to demonstrate rates of change. Early in the process, the BLROI asks participants to estimate the *probability* that they will change their behavior, *when* they anticipate changing, and *by how much*. In the middle of the process, the BLROI asks for estimates of actual change plus the continuing probability for more change. At the end of the process, the BLROI asks participants to estimate finally what actually *did* change in their behavior. This use of probability over time tracks the flow of change through an organization and guides management teams in ensuring that anticipated change becomes the change needed to reach ROI goals. It also engages participants in their own change management and creates more commitment to the change itself.

### Graphs: Seeing Behavior in Action

With these key concepts in mind, it is possible to show a sample graph that demonstrates an ideal interplay of learning curves and ROI growth. In any BLROI study, the two most important graphs are the performance *activity* graph and its corollary, a *benefits* graph isolated to the training intervention. A sample activity graph is shown in figure 3.

The BLROI data-collection points are known as the baseline (or precourse), postcourse, checkpoint(s), and final impact.

To draw a picture of behavior change, the first set of data must capture what participants are or believe they are doing before they are exposed to any new training program. This set of data is known as the participant baseline or "precourse" data. Immediately following the completion of a course, participants provide a new estimate

**Figure 3. Sample BLROI activity graph: total primary product sales.**

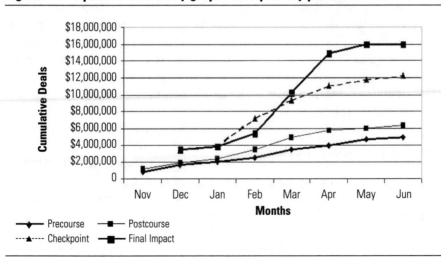

---

of what they believe they will and can do when they return to the job. In figure 3, the second line from the bottom—the line marked with smaller squares—is the postcourse estimate, and that estimate is important. When a group of participants give data on what they think they can do immediately after a class, they are really describing how fast they believe they can move through the early learning phase. The postcourse line is the equivalent of the surface view learning curve, or the trajectory of the early learners.

Because it is possible for performance to drop after a new training program until new behaviors are assimilated, this postcourse line can show how deep that drop will be and how long it will last before performance improves again. This estimate helps managers and trainers know how much additional reinforcement may be needed to keep an organization moving forward to meet its goals.

After some period back on the job, it is important to find out how the participants are doing. Checkpoints can be spaced days, weeks, or months apart, depending on how long it takes for performance change to appear. Checkpoint data begins to leverage both probability estimates and actual performance. In figure 3, one checkpoint is shown in the dashed line marked by triangles directly above the postcourse data. Notice that the checkpoint line is becoming more rounded and is beginning to approximate a bell curve.

The final impact data collection line reflects only the actual change achieved by the end of the study period. No probability estimates are included in the final data collection. This does not mean that the organization will stop accruing benefits from the training. The use of the term "final" only means that the benefits stop being measured. In figure 3, the solid line marked by larger squares represents the final impact data. Notice that the line resembles the shape of a bell curve. This curve reveals how long it took an organization to ramp up its learning and adoption and how close it came to achieving its ROI goals.

The primary benefit graph very closely resembles the activity graph, but has no precourse baseline. (Because the baseline benefit is zero, it is not useful to plot that line on a benefits graph.) The real difference is that activity graphs show all participant activity for the period, but benefit graphs show only the value that can be attributed to the training course itself. Depending on how data is collected, it's also possible to plot subsets of the benefit graphs. Benefit subsets are discussed in the next section below.

## Training Scorecard Application

Large-Tech had an aggressive goal to grow sales in the targeted key product area. According to leading industry analysts, the market for this product was growing at a rate of 25 percent to 30 percent per year. At the beginning of this study, Large-Tech believed its top competitor was growing 30 percent per year and its two next-largest competitors were experiencing flat or declining sales. Market share was a critical balanced scorecard metric for Large-Tech. The company's own annual sales quotas had established a 20 percent growth rate target for this key product.

In addition to its growth rate, Large-Tech had one other key metric to improve market share. On the average, Large-Tech sales representatives closed two to three deals a month for this product. Large-Tech won only 35 percent of these deals for which it competed with one or more other bidders. Large-Tech's senior managers refused to accept losing 65 percent of their deals. The expenses incurred to compete for the lost deals were a heavy burden on Large-Tech's cost of goods sold, gross profit margin, and net revenue. Its sales win percentage had to improve if the company were ever to meet its growth numbers and aggressively gain more market share. Large-Tech did not create a specific target to improve its win probability, but it definitely wanted to know if the financial selling course was helping its salesforce in this area.

The North American training department and sales management team selected a conservative 45 percent net Level 5 ROI to be achieved within 12 months. Because each class in the study was tracked for only six months, this goal was divided in half to create a 22.5 percent ROI goal to be achieved by each class within six months.

To determine ROI, establishing the total investment or the cost is required. Large-Tech's training investment was fully loaded with all standard accounting and purchasing costs, as well as the sales opportunity cost for the loss of the time the sales representatives took to travel to the class site and to attend the class itself. Costs also included estimates for the real dollars to be spent in gathering data for the ROI study and the value of the time sales staff would take to respond to each request for data.

To cover the class costs and make the 22.5 percent ROI goal in six months, it was estimated that each Large-Tech sales representative needed to bring in an additional *net* $126,000 that they would not have been able to sell without taking this course in financial selling.

But no training course can ever take 100 percent credit for all new sales that occur immediately thereafter. The North American sales manager estimated that only about 25 percent of additional sales would be credited to the course. That expectation meant that the *gross* benefit that each sales representative would have to bring in was an additional $504,000 in six months. The North American sales manager felt that if those numbers could be achieved, then this course would have made a significant contribution to Large-Tech's growth goals.

## Data Collection

Table 1 summarizes class locations, dates, participants, and completed phases. Data was collected four times for each class. The first data point, the participant baseline, was gathered from the participants in the five minutes before their class started. This data point is labeled "Precourse" in Large-Tech's graphs. The second data point was gathered at the end of the two-day class before participants left the session. The second data point is labeled "Postcourse" in Large-Tech's graphs. The third data collection or "Checkpoint" was performed three months after the class. In Large-Tech's graphs, "Checkpoint" is labeled "Action." The fourth or "Final Impact" data collection occurred six months after the class.

## Selection of the Graphs

In addition to the summary activity graph discussed above, Large-Tech chose to track five other types of activity graphs. They also wanted a summary benefit graph and three subset benefit graphs for each class. Large-Tech also received breakeven rate and adoption rate graphs for each class.

## Table 1. Class Summary

| Location | Dates | Number of Participants | Last Completed Phase |
|----------|-------|------------------------|----------------------|
| California | November, 2001 | 8 | Final Impact |
| Northeast1 | February, 2002 | 8 | Checkpoint |
| Midwest | March, 2002 | 14 | Checkpoint |
| Northeast2 | April, 2002 | 9 | Post-Class |

Large-Tech's six activity graphs were
- primary product sales
- additional sales leverage (add-on sales of other products leveraged from target or primary product in the study)
- current relationships (within the customer account)
- average deal size (for the primary or target product)
- average discount
- sales cycle time (average time to close a sale).

A sample of the activity graphs from the first (California) class is shown in figure 4. Some interesting things to note in the graphs for this class are that the original baseline, postcourse estimates, and checkpoint data lines all stayed very close to each other over time. The sales cycle time leapt to a very high level at checkpoint (or action), but dropped back down at final impact. Average deal size did increase by the end of the study of this class. Add-on sales of other products (shown as additional product leverage) had higher activity in the final phase of the study for this class. Customer relationships appear to have moved higher.

Remember, however, that these graphs simply show trends in activity. It is inappropriate to assume just yet that the class created any positive or negative trends in this data. The important thing is to note the trends for comparison with the information shown in the benefit graphs.

Large-Tech's four benefit graphs were
- total benefits
- additional primary product sold
- additional product leverage (add-on sales of other products leveraged from target or primary product in the study)
- win probability (how likely the sales representative was to win the deal).

Large-Tech's benefit graphs differ from their activity graphs for three reasons. Large-Tech's highest priority focused on sales growth and percentage of deals won, and those two metrics are tracked in their four benefit graphs. The benefit impact in the data that is not shown (sales cycle time and average discounts) was too small to graph. It was also decided that win probability had more impact simply as a benefit graph. There were some inverse correlations between longer sales cycle time and higher win probability that were opposite of what was expected. This could best be explained by showing sales cycle time in an activity graph, comparing it to win probability as a benefit and using some of the best-practice stories to shed light on certain

# Figure 4. Sample activity graphs from Large-Tech's first training class.

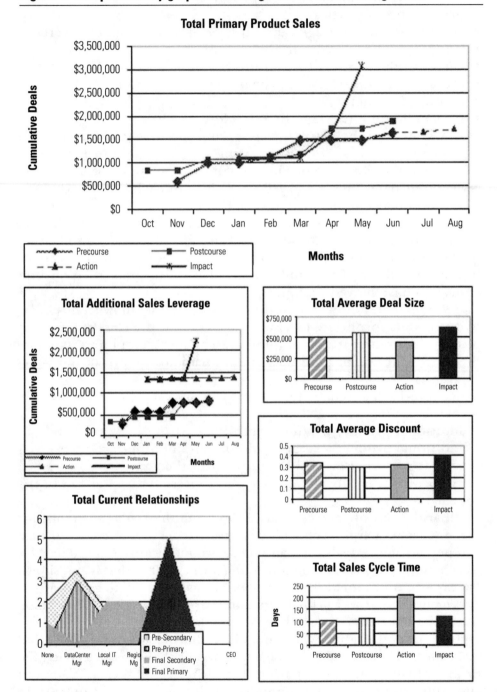

situations where such an inverse correlation was actually *good* for Large-Tech's chances to win.

A sample of the benefit graphs from the first (California) class is shown in figure 5.

The summary benefit graph shows that the class does have rapidly escalating benefits in the final data collection phase. The subset graphs demonstrate their value by highlighting which performance areas generated the greatest benefit for Large-Tech. The first subset graph shows a very slight benefit in increased sales of the target product. The second subset graph showing the benefit to add-on sales leverage is blank because no benefit was isolated to this area. The overwhelming benefit in this first class was in dramatically increasing the win probability or the chance that the sales representatives would win their deals.

### Phase I Findings: The Early Learners

Unfortunately, during the first part of this study Large-Tech's sales management team experienced a sweeping reorganization. The sales managers were not able to focus their attention on early reinforcement of the training. This situation split the study into a Phase I—before reinforcement—and Phase II—after reinforcement arrangement.

PHASE I BENEFIT ANALYSIS. Because each class size was so small, Large-Tech had to be cautious about the trends seen in any one class. When the classes were examined together, however, it was clear that the financial selling class was making a notable impact. This class significantly improved win probability. Sales representatives gave credit for an average 36 percent higher probability to win their deals, with an average of 82 percent confidence in their estimates. Improving win probability was a key strategy in support of Large-Tech's balanced scorecard market growth metric.

Examining best practices of the early learners showed that the techniques from this class were even able to turn around deals that were within minutes of being lost. This *increased* the sales cycle time for the deals where Large-Tech was fighting to turn the deal in their favor, but was considered a benefit for win probability. This explained the initial increase in sales cycle time shown on the activity graphs.

In looking across all classes, the benefits of lowered discounts, larger deal sizes, and larger add-on sales appear to be positive, although not as dramatic as the win probability benefits. These trends need more time and more supporting data before the training department can confidently claim them as true course benefits. The sales representatives

# Figure 5. Sample benefit graphs from Large-Tech's first training class.

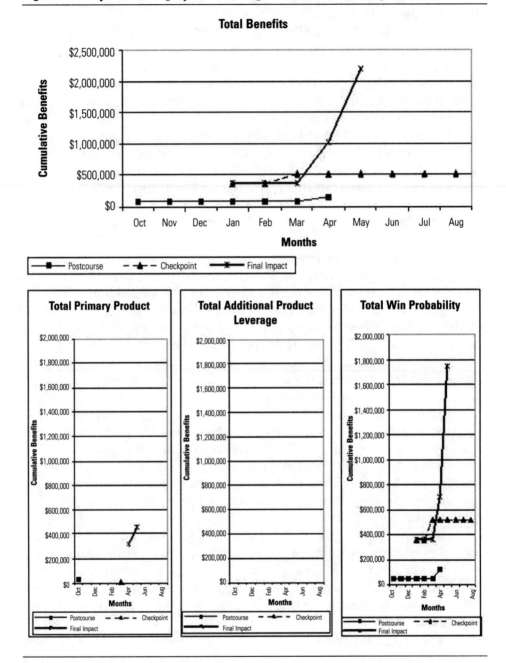

seem to be building higher customer relationships, but because the data was not collected in such a way as to validate and isolate this relationship to the class, Large-Tech can view this only as a possible intangible benefit of the course.

ROI. The ROI from the first (California) class finished at 330 percent. A graph of Large-Tech's breakeven and ROI analysis is shown in figure 6. The straight line across the graph is the cost estimate for the training program and ROI study. The financial return from the class must meet that line in order for the class to have recovered all of its costs. The return from the class must meet the ROI goal in order for the training program to be considered successful.

The trajectory from the initial postcourse participant estimate to the ROI goal was plotted to show the managers how much more in sales needed to be brought in and how quickly that needed to happen during the six months of the study for this class. The trajectory of what had been gained and what remained to be gained to meet the ROI goal was replotted at the checkpoint and final data-gathering phases. These graphs enable the managers of the participants in a class to see the ROI progress of that class at a glance.

**Figure 6. California class breakeven analysis.**

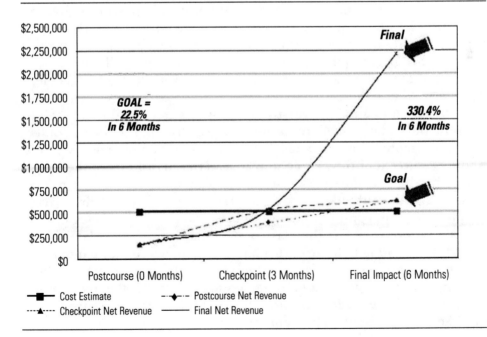

What was even more interesting was that the breakeven and ROI trends from the three other classes still in progress are very different from the California class. The current breakeven and ROI projections from the class participants are shown in figure 7. The Northeast1 class appears to be losing even more ROI at checkpoint. The Midwest class seems to be set to create phenomenal returns, even better than the California class. The Northeast2 class is the only one to even project a positive ROI immediately following the class. Large-Tech's managers are very interested in finding out how they can reach the breakeven point for each class more quickly and consistently and how they can create and maintain a higher and more consistent ROI trend line for each class.

LEARNING CURVE. One aspect of Large-Tech's graphs may help managers understand how to create a quick, consistent breakeven and ROI for each class. The second or postcourse line is the indication of the early learners' confidence in their ability to assimilate new skills and of how quickly they believe they will grow their performance. In Large-Tech's case, postcourse estimates significantly differed from precourse estimates for two of three classes, one dropping quite steeply. The scorecard in figure 7 summarizes the learning curve gaps between pre- and postcourse estimates. Figure 8 is a sample graph, from Large-Tech's fourth class (Northeast2), depicting this type of pre- and postcourse gap. In the example, the drop was about $4 million or −16 percent. Based on three pre- and postcourse estimates combined with the behavior patterns from the three classes that have gone to the checkpoint stage or further, this graph is interpreted to mean that there is likely to be a *higher* ROI from the participants in this class, with less reinforcement needed to obtain it.

Data on how adopters versus nonadopters estimated their deals at the postcourse data collection showed two key findings. Future adopters were much more likely to change their predictions than were nonadopters. About 80 percent of the people who *adopted* raised or lowered their postcourse prediction of their performance to a point either much greater than or significantly less than their original estimate. In three cases, adopters would not give a new postclass prediction even after being pressed for one before they left the classroom. This behavior was later interpreted as indicating that the participant was mentally committed to adoption, but was not yet clear on his or her goals and was unwilling to submit meaningless data. But even more intriguing was that 100 percent of the people who did *not adopt* did not change their postcourse prediction or changed it by a very small amount.

# Figure 7. Large-Tech's financial selling course Bottom-Line ROI training scorecard as of June 3, 2002.

| Class/# of Participants | Total Goal — 38 (Status) | California — 8 (Final) | Northeast1 — 8 (Checkpoint) | Midwest — 13 (Checkpoint) | Northeast2 — 9 (Post-Class) |
|---|---|---|---|---|---|
| **ROI** *(six month basis)* | | Value | Value | Value | Value |
| Post | -22.5% | -69.56% [?] | -65.03% [?] | -77.20% [?] | 11.03% [☑] |
| Check | 0% | 3.72% [☑] | -78.29% [☒] | 346.03% [☑] | |
| Final | *22.5%* | *330.40%* [☑] | | | |
| **Benefits** | | Value (Confidence) | Value (Confidence) | Value (Confidence) | Value (Confidence) |
| Win Probability | 20% | *53.75% (71.88)* [☑] | 15.0% (77.5) [?] | 20.83% (88.75) [☑] | |
| Product Sales | | *$616,822 (85.0)* [☑] | $56,000 (100¹) [☒] | $909,320 (80") [☑] | |
| Solution Leverage | | $0 [☒] | $0 [☒] | $535,500 (90") [☑] | |
| % Less Discount | 5% | 0% [☒] | 0% [☒] | 7.5% (40%) [?] | |
| Cycle Time | -10% | 0%² [☒] | 0% [☒] | -15.24% (41.43) [?] | |
| **Payback** *(Predicted vs. Actual Start)* | | Value | Value | Value | Value |
| Post | *4 weeks* | 5 weeks [?] | 3 weeks [☑] | 4 weeks [☑] | 3 weeks [☑] |
| Check | *10 weeks* | *9 weeks* | *8 weeks* [☑] | 13 weeks [?] | |
| Final | *10 weeks* | *9 weeks* | *8 weeks* [☑] | | |

## Best Practices

Confidence to Take the Customer to Higher Numbers & Higher Value, Moving Purchase to "Right Now," Forcing Competition into "Price" to Win, Roadmap Strategy, Throwing Out the Incumbent, Prepping Reseller

**Summary:** Financial Selling class appears to return a positive ROI, but results vary widely among classes. It is possible to drive the ROI from this class much higher using consistent focus and reinforcement from the sales management team and more emphasis on sharing the best practices of the top performers so that the average performers can quickly raise their sales skills by following the same path. Gaining management team involvement will be the key to creating more consistency in final ROI numbers.

## Key Issues

Clear communication: short vs. long-term pressure for sales, mid-market examples, quick "cheat sheets" and tools, make research faster, make peer experts available, get managers through program so they can reinforce, use real deals in class case studies

| | Total Goal | California | Northeast1 | Midwest | Northeast2 |
|---|---|---|---|---|---|
| Learning Curve Gap | 66% | +6% [☑] | 0% [☑] | (Invalid Data) | -16% [☑] |
| Adoption Rate | | 50% (4 of 8) [?] | 25% (2 of 8) [☒] | 38% (5 of 13) [?] | |

**Legend:** ☑ = Acceptable/Good Value; ? = Caution/Questionable Poor Value; ☒ = Unacceptable Poor Value; ***Bold Italic*** = Goal or Final Study Value; Normal Text = Value for Current Stage of an In-Progress ROI Study

¹Note: Confidence factor rating from only one participant
²One extreme value of 100% in sales cycle time not shown

**Figure 8. Northeast2 learning curve.**

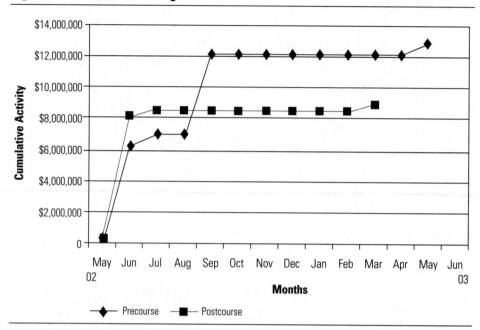

Given these patterns, this would indicate that the greater the difference in the pre- and postclass estimates, the *more* committed the participants in the class were to using the skills back on the job. Regardless of whether it was predicted in the pre- and postcourse estimates, it is likely that performance would drop initially for adopters. The fact that some participants seem to accept and predict change and that some seem not to accept it and predict no change tells us how much reinforcement and follow-up may be needed with a group to reach the target ROI more quickly and consistently.

ADOPTION RATE. The adoption rate graphs also will help Large-Tech achieve its target ROI more rapidly and consistently. The scorecard in table 1 summarizes the adoption rates for each class, and figure 9 presents the adoption rate graph from the third (Midwest) class. In that graph, the dark gray area shows the potential if there was 100 percent adoption (that is, if 13 people adopted). The light gray area shows current adoption (five people). The black area shows nonresponsive people (five). Given the pattern of response across all classes, from the nonresponders it would be expected that only one or two actually might have adopted; the others have done so. The ideal picture would have been to have the dark gray area completely covered with light gray instead.

**Figure 9. Graph of the Midwest adoption rate.**

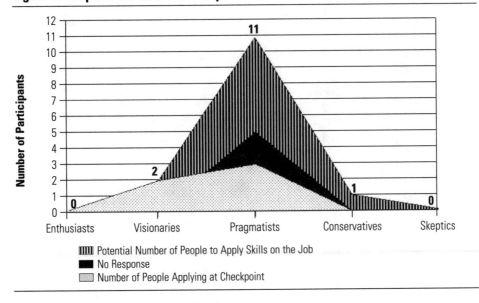

The average adoption rate from the three classes that had made it through their checkpoint and final stages was 33 percent. With so much room for more adoption, Large-Tech's sales managers immediately realized their ROI could be even higher.

PAYBACK. Large-Tech is focused on one more way to reach breakeven and their ROI goals more quickly. Data from the three classes that have passed the checkpoint phase (figure 10) reveals that representatives consistently predict impact to start approximately one month after the class. The checkpoint data, however, shows that the first improvement in a sale attributable to this class consistently occurs eight to 13 weeks after the class.

If Large-Tech can reduce the time before payback starts, it will realize internal rate of return benefits on cashflow more quickly than it otherwise might have done. In addition, understanding the payback pattern for this class can help sales managers decide which people could benefit the most from this course, when they should attend, and when the effects of having attended should begin to appear back on the job.

SCORECARD. Large-Tech's performance is summarized in figure 7 where measurements taken with the BLROI process are shown in the scorecard. Because the learning curve gap and adoption rates appear

**Figure 10. Payback analysis from the California class.**

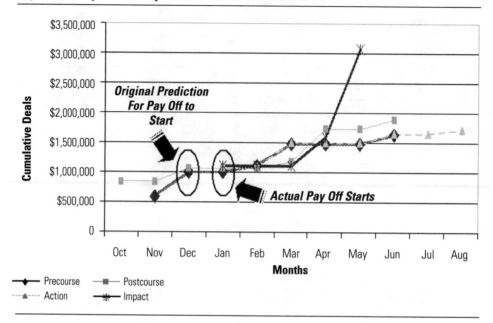

to foreshadow ROI, these are compared to target goals at the top of the scorecard. ROI for each class is then listed by study phase. The benefits driving the ROI are shown next. Average predicted and actual payback times are listed below the benefits. Best practices and key issues are then summarized. A current study status is summarized at the bottom of the scorecard.

### Phase II: Crossing the Chasm

In the next three months of the study, the North American sales manager wants his organization to double the adoption rate from one-third to two-thirds of the participants. Following future classes, he also wants to see if his organization can shorten the start of the payback period by a minimum of two weeks to a total of six or eight weeks.

The most important issue to address was the conflicting messages that sales managers were sending to their people. Many representatives reported that the short-term pressure from sales managers to close deals was so great that they could not risk a drop in their performance, even if the long-term gain would be substantial. Other suggestions for improvement included providing better tools and examples, requiring all sales managers to take the course, and making peer experts available for quick advice.

During their BLROI study, adopters provided best practices, which will transfer into examples and tools. These best practices will be shared in audio conferences. The next update of the course will include these cases as well. In looking back at figure 2 in this case study, updating the class itself is part of the standardize step after crossing the chasm. Large-Tech's sales team is working on a standard reinforcement plan that all of the firstline managers will use with their sales representatives who attend this course.

## Communicating Results

One-on-one meetings and teleconferences have proved to be the most effective means for communicating results. The North American product training manager and her boss, the sales training section manager, held monthly progress reviews to keep current on this project. In addition, the North American sales training manager held a quarterly staff meeting for her section managers six months into the study. Status presentations have been given to North American sales managers. The data gathered so far is so compelling that additional reviews within the sales and training organizations are being planned.

An initial status update report was written, showing pre- and post-course data from the first (California) class, issues, recommendations, and breakeven points. The author gave the target product's worldwide sales manager an early presentation to explain the study in the North American region. Supported by the first written status report, this presentation was given two months after the study had begun. This early report also has been shared with Large-Tech's European and Asian sales training managers.

## Lessons Learned

- This methodology is so new that every audience had to be educated before they understood their graphs and their responsibilities. Trying to speed up the process by cutting the education short always ended up taking more time in the end. Education must be thoroughly and well done if the rest of the study is to go smoothly.
- Involving first- and second-level managers early was very important, but it would have been more credible to wait to communicate with the worldwide or third-level manager until actual data was available later in the study.
- This type of study rapidly can turn into a way of life. The potential for driving the business in new ways is so intriguing that the

more data the study provided, the more data managers wanted and the more classes they wanted to include.

- The sequencing, timing, and content presented strongly influenced how the audience reacted to it. It is important to help managers think creatively about what the data means and how they can use it to help themselves. Encourage creativity.
- Audiences wanted many views of the data based on demographics, such as years of experience or location. Demographic data should be built into the surveys.
- Maintaining neutrality and trust and treating sensitive information confidentially proved vital to getting reliable data and achieving the goals of the study.
- The simple act of gathering data is a powerful motivator for people to want to do well. What gets measured, gets done!
- The best salespeople are ruthless in their time management. It took time and a great deal of persistence to get data, but it was well worth the effort. Don't give up!

## Questions for Discussion

1. Sales is one of the easiest areas in which to apply this methodology because it is easier to trace activity, impact, and ROI. What are some other business areas where this methodology would prove relatively easy to apply?

2. How would you apply this methodology to other skills training or with different training media, such as e-learning? Leadership training?

3. Does an organization have to have a balanced scorecard for this methodology to be valuable? Why or why not? What advantages would this methodology leverage in an organization that does have a balanced scorecard in place?

4. How does this methodology improve the ability of a training department or vendor to provide performance consulting to a line organization?

5. If this methodology were to be applied consistently over several skill programs or over a longer period (for example, one to two years), how could this help an organization's competitive planning process?

## The Author

Theresa L. Seagraves is president and CEO of Theresa L. Seagraves & Associates. Her firm specializes in productivity analysis and training and development ROI. She developed the BLROI. As a former training manager in a *Fortune* 100 corporation, Seagraves helped her organizations earn top honors and recognition as the best performers in their industry. She is a regular speaker on ROI and evaluation topics at industry conferences. Her firm is located near Denver, Colorado. She can be reached at 303.840.5102 or at tseagraves@drive-roi.com.

## Acknowledgment
The author would like to acknowledge Stephen Kirkpatrick of Denver's Regis University for his special assistance in conversations and reviews and for his suggestions on early drafts of this case study.

## References
Kaplan, Robert S., and David P. Norton. (1996). *The Balanced Scorecard: Translating Strategy into Action.* Boston: Harvard Business School Press.

Moore, Geoffrey A. (1999). *Crossing the Chasm: Marketing and Selling High-Tech Products to Mainstream Customers.* New York: HarperCollins.

Moore, Geoffrey A. (1995). *Inside the Tornado: Marketing Strategies from Silicon Valley's Cutting Edge.* New York: HarperBusiness.

Phillips, Jack J. (1997). *Return on Investment in Training and Performance Improvement Programs.* Boston: Butterworth-Heinemann.

# Learning Services: Implementing a Training Scorecard to Demonstrate Value

## The Mellear Corporation

Stephanie Barber and Patricia Albaugh

*The Mellear Corporation is a large service organization in an extremely competitive industry. There is a strong emphasis on profitability measures, particularly in the area of expense reduction. Similar to many companies, the functional areas of the business that do not directly produce revenue are often prime targets for these cost reduction efforts. Mellear's Learning Services organization has employed a scorecard approach to begin to quantify and demonstrate the value of its services. This approach has helped build and strengthen partnerships within the business. These efforts and the supporting processes are critical components of the goal to become more business centered and more closely aligned with business priorities.*

In late 2001 and early 2002, the training organization supported a critical sales initiative. This sales initiative and its related learning program were highly visible to senior leaders because the results could have a significant impact on sales revenue. This learning program was used as a pilot for developing and testing the current scorecard practices and methodology. In this case study, the training program is used as a successful example of training's impact on business results and the use of these results in communication with senior business leaders and line managers.

The industry has been extremely competitive and it has been marked by overinvestment and debt. Traditional products and services within this industry are experiencing significant decline as a

*This case was prepared to serve as a basis for discussion rather than to illustrate either effective or ineffective administrative and management practices. Names of places, organizations, or people have been disguised at the request of the author or organization.*

result of competition, overcapacity, and technology replacement. However, there are profitable growth segments that require the combination of leading-edge technology and a reliable, stable infrastructure.

At the time of this publication, the industry is fiercely competitive and turbulent. Most of the major players are experiencing severe financial difficulty, including credit rating downgrades and bankruptcies. In this period of decline and consolidation, an opportunity exists to emerge as a dominant player within the profitable growth segments. The success of this corporation depends on its ability to capitalize on these new segments and equip its workforce with needed new skills in a short period of time.

Historically, training organization members have not been proactive in identifying and implementing improvements in areas that may either maximize the current resources and investments or that may reduce costs. Over the last six months, the business has reorganized and consolidated Learning Services (LS) within specific segments of the business. The resulting target audiences and supported segments will become increasingly diverse. Simultaneously, cost targets will have to be maintained or exceeded in accordance with a business-restructuring plan.

Under new leadership within the training organization, there is a renewed emphasis on instilling a business-centric mindset and producing profitable, value-added programs. For many people within the organization, this is a paradigm shift from being a culture of "all things to all people" to being solely focused on supporting business priorities. The perception of training is changing from a sense of individual entitlement to an activity driven by business goals. In accordance with this paradigm shift, the training team is becoming increasingly more cognizant and proactive about identifying potential areas for maximizing current resources and investments or for reducing cost.

The LS organization published its first quarterly scorecard in spring 2002. The scorecard, a collection of outcome-based metrics aligned with each of the business objectives for this year, is intended to capture business results and outcomes and provide a snapshot of LS's value to the business. Each of the training leaders was responsible for aligning learning services activities to support or drive the desired business results and outcomes. As the organization expands, LS will include more business objectives and the appropriate metrics.

## Training Scorecard Methodology

Over the last year, the training leaders explored various scorecard models. Some team members participated in the Balanced Scorecard

Collaborative Action Working Group. A balanced training scorecard was proposed initially as the appropriate starting point for the measurement endeavor. A balanced scorecard typically includes four types of metrics: financial, customer satisfaction, operations, and learning/growth (Kaplan and Norton, 1996). Ultimately, the senior leaders chose a more simple, graphic view of a few strategic, outcome-based metrics. Instead of a dozen or more balanced metrics, the team wanted to use the measurement to reinforce the business-centric approach of remaining focused on a few critical and strategic programs. The original selections all had direct and substantial effects on the bottom line. The scorecard summary would capture the five levels of evaluation, as defined by Donald Kirkpatrick (1998) and Jack Phillips (1997), with primary emphasis on Levels 3 and 4 (behavioral change and business impact). Figure 1 depicts the scorecard designed by Mellear.

The decision to use a subset of very strategic business impact results was critical and successful. At the point of scorecard launch, the internal systems and resources did not exist to support a more robust or balanced view. The simplicity of the approach and the direct alignment with business priorities enabled more focused discussions around key business issues.

Organizational changes were instituted to support this approach. These changes included creating a position to coordinate the metrics, evaluation, and scorecard work across the entire LS organization (that is, the evaluation and metrics manager). An evaluation committee was created to establish the common processes and templates necessary to support measurement across the organization. In each team, an evaluation subject matter expert was responsible for supporting evaluation activities within the team's organization.

As part of the annual planning cycle, each director within the organization met with his or her respective business partners to identify the priorities for 2002. Whenever possible, these priorities included financial, operational, and customer satisfaction metrics. Training activities were proposed and aligned appropriately to support or drive the desired business results for each business priority. Information from these executive interviews was combined with funding model data, and the outputs were used to create a results-based budget for LS for the year.

Major activities and projects were aligned to each business priority, and owners were assigned to each. The directors met with the evaluation and metrics (EM) manager to identify appropriate quarterly metrics for monitoring progress and the outcomes generated through LS activities. Metrics were validated with the appropriate directors and

**Figure 1. Mellear's training scorecard.**

| | Level 1: Participant Reaction | Level 2: Learning | Level 3: Behavioral Change | Level 4: Business Impact | Level 5: ROI |
|---|---|---|---|---|---|
| Measurement methodology | Participant satisfaction; survey instrument administered at end of course | Comparison of precourse and postcourse test performance; precourse tests administered prior to attendance; postcourse tests administered at end of course | Sales tracking system; monthly results | Sales tracking system; monthly results; comparison group of nonparticipants used to distinguish results | Average sale closed generated $2,500; increase in leads $\times$ 25 percent success rate $\times$ participants<br><br>ROI = [(Revenue − Cost]/Cost] $\times$ 100 |
| Overall results | 3.8 out of 5 | 20.14 percent average increase in pre- and post-assessment scores<br><br>Precourse test success: 133; postcourse test success: 857 | Not tracked at the individual level; there was an overall increase in funnel activity consistent with the average lead increase per participant | Lead generation per participant: with training: 6.5; without training: 4.0 | Projected incremental revenue: $979,773; estimated cost: $582,727<br><br>ROI = 168 percent |

business owners. Within each organization, resources were identified to monitor and track these quarterly metrics.

The ardent sponsorship and support of the new LS vice president was a key success factor in the measurement efforts. The concept of aligning training activities with business priorities and measuring the outcomes relative to the bottom line was a consistent message in all forums. These communications were buoyed by the organization changes to support these measurement efforts, including resource and technology investments.

In preparation for the scorecard endeavor, the organization decided to use a highly visible, high-impact sales program as a pilot for proposed processes, methodologies, and communication efforts. This sales program and its effect on lead-generation is the focus of this paper.

## Training Scorecard Application

In accordance with shifts in the industry and competitive pressures, it became necessary for the company to become more dominant in a nontraditional segment. This growing segment required different types of selling skills and knowledge about nontraditional products and services. The shift from the traditional product and service sets to more robust solutions with newer products and services knowledge was critical to survival in the industry. The business identified the specifics of this new sales initiative and asked LS to provide the training to support it.

The line managers speculated that current sales were lacking in the new segment because account executives could not identify sales opportunities. This hypothesis was confirmed through needs analysis, and a training curriculum was created to align performance with expectations.

The target population was account executives (approximately 2,000) and their sales managers ( approximately 200). The business requested a program commensurate with the launch of the sales initiative. This resulted in an extremely compressed timeframe for design and deployment with a large, geographically dispersed target audience. Initially, learning program attendance was designed to be mandatory, but only half of the target audience attended the instructor-led session.

The analysis of the program focused on the account executives and their lead-generation performance. The lead performances of account executives who attended the instructor-led portion of the program were compared monthly with their counterparts who had not attended training. The results were summarized and presented to the senior leaders. The program was a compilation of related learning interventions, consisting of a one-day, leader-led classroom program and as many as nine supplemental Web-based programs.

This program was an obvious candidate for an impact study. The criticality of the skills sets to business priorities, the direct bottom-line effect of applying these skills, the high level of management interest, the size of the target audience, and the higher-than-average costs were contributing factors. Figure 2 presents the evaluation plan designed to identify the results of the training program.

The overall goal of this training program was to build confidence and competence around selling particular services across the product portfolio. The aligned training activities reflected in the score-card report generally indicate a favorable impact on business performance and business results. The majority of these results were obtained using descriptive statistics and, where applicable and appropriate, comparison group and trend analysis methodologies. These results included both activity-oriented metrics, such as the number of completions for each instructor-led and Web-based session, and outcome-based metrics, such as account executive lead performance.

The sales department provided the average monthly revenue and close rate for the major sales lead types (figure 3). This information was used to calculate the monetary value of the program. Comparison groups were established using data from the sales funnels combined with training activity data. A common identifier was used to correlate the data. Throughout the data collection process, members of the sales team were used as subject matter experts to validate the data. The outcome metrics shown in the final reports were based on data provided by the sales team. The training activity data was used merely to establish the samples (training attendees versus nontraining attendees by delivery mode).

The lead performances of trained account executives and of their nontrained counterparts were compared on a monthly basis by delivery mode (figure 4). A trend analysis compared the historical lead performances of the account executives in each population for the instructor-led training. These results isolated the impact of the training program using a comparison group methodology. The executive summary included the average leads per account executive for training participants and for those who did not attend training. At the conclusion of the program, training attendees had an average of 2.5 more leads than did their nonparticipating counterparts.

**Figure 2. Mellear's evaluation plan.**

| Evaluation Level | Objectives | Data Source | Data Items | Timing |
|---|---|---|---|---|
| **Level 4— business impact** | • Increase qualified services leads resulting in sales of related products and services<br>• Generate a minimum of three customer proposals for these products and services | Sales tracking system | • Number of leads generated<br>• Number of proposals generated | One to three months after learning event |
| **Level 3— application and performance objectives** | • Develop and execute action plans for a minimum of 10 customer contacts<br>• Engage customers in an interview to uncover opportunities specific to these products and services<br>• Team with appropriate resources to maximize potential for closing the opportunity | Sales tracking system | • Number of prospective clients (prospects)<br>• Progress of prospects<br>• Number of referrals | Two to four weeks after learning event |
| **Level 2— learning objectives** | • Explain why specific products and services are important to company success<br>• Identify the services that constitute the product and services portfolios<br>• Articulate the value of product and services to a customer<br>• Ask the appropriate probing questions to identify a potential sales opportunity<br>• Discuss how ROI can increase with specific product and services | Pre- and postprogram assessments | Comparison of assessment scores | Conclusion of learning event |
| **Level 1— participant reaction and planned action** | Employee positive reaction to:<br>• content relevancy to job<br>• delivery<br>• meeting objectives<br>• overall satisfaction<br>• deliverables<br>• relevance of precourse requirements | Participant survey | Threshold four out of five points | Conclusion of learning event |

Evaluation levels source: Jack Phillips (1997).

## Figure 3. Weekly sales department report.

| Projected Monthly Revenue and Sales Leads | | | |
|---|---|---|---|
| Projected Revenue | Percentage Change over Prior Week | Number of Sales Leads | Percentage Change over Prior Week |
| $58,500,00 | + 26.50 | 2,600 | + 71.15 |

Note: Figures are for illustrative purposes only and do not reflect actual results.

| Participant Feedback (Phillips/Kirkpatrick Level 1) | |
|---|---|
| *Sample Size* | *1,000* |
| **Participant Feedback Category** | **Average** |
| **Job relevance** | **4.22** |
| I am confident that I will be able to apply this session to my job. | 4.41 |
| The knowledge I gained during this session will have a significant impact on my job performance. | 3.85 |
| **Course content** | **3.86** |
| The materials presented were accurate and complete. | 4.17 |
| **Instructor effectiveness** | **4.45** |
| The instructor was able to provide real-world insight based on his/her experiences. | 4.43 |
| The instructor explained the subject matter clearly. | 4.51 |
| **Course structure** | **4.15** |
| The materials corresponded well to what was taught in the course. | 4.18 |
| The session used enough hands-on case studies or role plays. | 4.17 |
| **Overall, I would rate this course as:** | **3.80** |

Note: Figures are for illustrative purposes only and do not reflect actual results.

Cost estimates and data were collected for this program. Although the return-on-investment (ROI) estimates were favorable, the business impact results were used to demonstrate the value of the program. The training leaders decided that the ROI for this program distracted audiences by creating some skepticism about the size of the ROI (168 percent) (tables 1 and 2). Instead of introducing skepticism into these powerful results, the business impact results were used as the primary vehicles for establishing the value of training services. The ROI data was used as supporting data and it was presented only on request.

**Figure 3. Weekly sales department report (continued).**

| Precourse Test Results | | |
|---|---|---|
| Category | Number of Students | Percentage Change from Prior Week |
| **Students passed and completed** <br> *A student confirmation indicates the student has completed and passed the program exam.* | 133 | 16 |
| **Students failed** <br> *A student attempted the exam and his or her score was not higher than 80 percent.* | 854 | 12 |
| **Students canceled** <br> *A student canceled the pretest for the program.* | 13 | 11 |
| Postcourse Test Results | | |
| Category | Number of Students | Percentage Change from Prior Week |
| **Students completed** | 857 | 24 |
| **Students failed** | 133 | 10 |
| **Students canceled** | 10 | 9 |

Note: Figures are for illustrative purposes only and do not reflect actual results.

## Communicating Results

The measurement efforts surrounding this program and the larger scorecard efforts represented a substantial change for the training organization and for other parts of the business. Internal and external communications were critical components of the efforts to broaden the business-centric mindset within training and effectively illustrate the value of learning services. This particular program was communicated at several levels within the organization. The training director of the products and services center of excellence held weekly reviews with the key business stakeholders. Those stakeholders routinely reviewed the progress of their particular organization. During the program, the line managers were focused largely on the number of account

## Figure 4. Executive summary: comparison of lead performance and training attendance.

| Account Executive Lead Performance and Training Attendance | Instructor-Led Program |
|---|---|
| Attended training | 6.50 |
| Did not attend training: average leads per account executive | 4.00 |
| Average lead difference | 2.50 |
| Percentage difference in number of leads by training attendees | 60 |
| Average monthly revenue per lead, overall | $2,500 |
| Potential value of leads (average lead difference × average monthly revenue per lead) | $6,250 |
| Estimated monthly close rate (conservative) | 25% |
| Potential monthly revenue differential per attendee | $1,563 |

Note: Figures are for illustrative purposes only and do not reflect actual results.

## Table 1. Cost categories.

| Cost Categories | Estimated Costs ($) |
|---|---|
| **Fixed costs (estimated)** | |
| Design and development | 26,131 |
| Additional resources | 1,307 |
| Total fixed costs (estimated) | 27,438 |
| **Variable costs (estimated)** | |
| Training operations and administration | 11,759 |
| Materials | 39,197 |
| Delivery | 104,525 |
| Evaluation and reporting | 7,839 |
| Participant costs | 391,969 |
| **Total variable costs (estimated)** | **555,289** |
| **Total cost of program** | **582,727** |
| Cost per participant | 583 |

Note: Figures are for illustrative purposes only and do not reflect actual results.

**Table 2. Program and quarterly ROI.**

| Projected Return | Instructor-Led Program |
|---|---|
| Total projected revenue difference for training attendees | $1,562,500 |
| Total estimated program costs for training attendees | $582,727 |
| Estimated potential revenue—estimated cost | $979,773 |
| Estimated potential revenue to estimated cost ratio | 1.68 |
| Estimated ROI | 168% |
| **If All Attended Training and Achieved Universal Benefit** | **Instructor-Led Program** |
| Potential revenue difference per attendee | $1,563 |
| Target additional account executives/agents to complete training requirements | 2000 |
| Potential additional revenue (if all attended training and achieved universal benefits) | $3,126,000 |
| Cost per account executive | $583 |
| Additional cost to train account executives | $1,165,454 |
| Estimated potential revenue—estimated cost | $1,960,546 |
| Estimated potential revenue to estimated cost ratio | 1.68 |
| Estimated ROI | 168% |

executives attending the sessions and accessing the Web-based training courses, and on the results of assessment exams. These reports enabled midcourse corrections. For example, the number of account executives taking the final exam was extremely low. The results were reviewed with the line managers and a decision was made to send out additional communications. The following weeks showed a dramatic increase in the number of participants completing the final exam. Report metrics that were lower than expected led to the development of a tool for the sales managers to use in tracking the students' participation in learning events. The feedback was positive; the senior managers were pleased, not only with the results but also with the information provided on the report.

As the program progressed, the vice president of learning services presented the executive summary to the senior sales leaders to review the progress of the program. Initially, these leaders were extremely surprised that the training organization had quantifiable data with bottom-line impact, but that surprise quickly turned to skepticism about the size of the impact. This skepticism was mitigated with supplemental data and secondary analyses. The executives found the combination of the comparison groups and the historical trend analysis significantly more compelling than either data set in isolation. A simple, graphic depiction of the most compelling results was developed for presentations and discussions with executives and line managers (figure 5). The intent was to create a picture that told the story at a glance. This easy-to-read synopsis has proved to be the most effective means of expression; it has been incorporated into multiple presentations for line managers, executives, and other internal training presentations (figure 6).

The results also were used to make decisions regarding training. At the time of this publication, a secondary analysis has been requested by executives to assess the close rates of the training participants versus nonparticipants. This information also will be used internally to assess the duration of the impact and whether the duration is dependent on delivery mode. Analysis of these results will guide decisions around

**Figure 5. Historical comparison of lead performance and training attendance.**

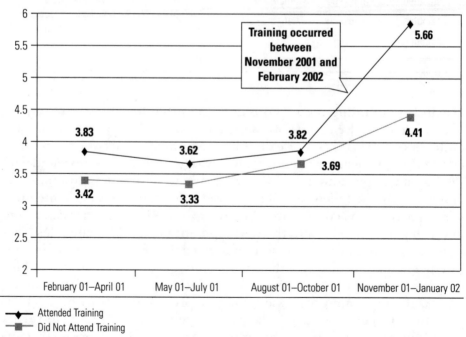

Note: Figures are for illustrative purposes only and do not reflect actual results.

**Figure 6. Program and quarterly ROI estimated return analysis.**

| | |
|---|---|
| **Projected Average Annual Revenue Difference for Training Attendees** | **$** |
| **Projected Average Quarterly Revenue Difference for Training Attendees**<br><br>Number of Training Attendees (2000) × Monthly Projected Average Revenue Difference ($5,647.50) × 3 months | **$33,885,000** |
| **Estimated Annual Costs of Training Program** | **$** |
| **Total Estimated Costs**<br><br>Number of Account Executives/Agents Attended Program<br>Estimated Cost Per Account Executive/Agent | **$1,445,701**<br><br>2000<br>$722.85 |

the development of future programs, especially with regard to the appropriate blending of solution and duration.

Within the training organization, these results were used consistently as an example of the outcome-based, business impact reports desired on an ongoing basis. These results were communicated to the training organization as a tool to reinforce the need for alignment between training activity and business priorities. These reports were used to illustrate the distinction between outcome-based metrics and traditional training activity metrics. These communications packages also were used during virtual brown-bag sessions to educate new training team members on measurement efforts.

## Lessons Learned

- The criticality of the evaluation planning and data-planning phase and its execution cannot be overemphasized. Evaluation planning was not incorporated into the initial phases because this program was developed rapidly. In fact, the decision to conduct a business impact study was made after the initial delivery of some courses. As a consequence, processes were not established up front to ensure the timely and accurate collection of all data required. Rectifying some of these problems was very resource and labor intensive. For example, rosters did not include the necessary identifier to link training participants with sales data. Ultimately, it was an extremely arduous process to look up and fill in thousands of identifiers. As a result of this experience, the process for collecting instructor-led rosters has been improved. Another example of a problem encountered is that action plans were a key component of the learning program and the sole indicators for assessing the application of skills. The action plans were not monitored until a critical juncture, and at that time it was discovered that the data had been corrupted.

- From a process perspective, it is critical to incorporate evaluation and data planning into the workflow for needs analysis and course design. As a result of this experience, online templates were developed to capture and document requisite information.
- The student reaction surveys (Level 1) were not customized for this program. Ideally, these reaction surveys would have included a planned action section that captured participants' predicted ability to perform by objective. This would have reinforced the linkage between the training program and the business result (lead generation). This data also would have provided a comparison point for the business impact study. Additionally, it would have been extremely helpful to have the students indicate the amount of time spent on Web-based training and to note whether these courses were taken during business hours or after hours. This information would be valuable for capturing cost data. The participant's time spent away from the job during business hours has an opportunity cost to the business; these estimates were incorporated in the overall costs. As well, this information would have been interesting from a corporate learning culture perspective.
- There was not sufficient time to consider the use of a management survey to supplement business impact data. A manager survey to assess participants' application of the learning objectives and/or a template to capture the action plan data would have been appropriate. Results from the manager surveys could have provided supporting data for the business impact report. Also, additional planning could have eliminated the use of several resources by allowing enough lead time to automate reports and integrate processes.
- The system infrastructure and subsequent process infrastructure were not in place to support these efforts because this type of analysis was new to the organization. At this time, the organization is moving rapidly to rectify these problems by integrating systems and creating more robust reporting tools.
- The use of actual business results was critical to the credibility of the data. As we continue to use actual performance data, such as

lead-generation performance, it will be increasingly important to understand the timeframes affiliated with sales cycles. Each product or offer has differing levels of complexity, both between the different products and within the individual products, which alter the time lag from sales proposal to revenue realization. It is important for the training organization to compare training activity and performance result at appropriate times. Additionally, it would have been helpful to collect baseline information prior to the program.

- An additional timing consideration was the time and resource necessary to understand the data sources, various sales funnels, and idiosyncrasies of this data. It was necessary to engage the use of a subject matter expert within the sales community to validate the sales funnel data. The sales leads are input by account executives and sales managers and, consequently, the product and service descriptions lack consistency. This subject matter expert had to manually identify the products and services affiliated specifically with this sales initiative—an extremely labor-intensive and inefficient process. This is another evaluation and data planning issue that could have been resolved up front with improved planning.

- Arrangements for collecting data, including alerting support resources, identifying appropriate systems and sources, and ensuring that data collection occurred regularly, should occur early in the report definition process. This did not happen and was a major source of difficulty in development of this business impact study. For example, the cost data for this program was captured after the program was completed. Although information was collected for all cost categories, the majority of the submissions were estimates. Extensive resource use could have been avoided by defining the evaluation requirements at the correct time in the front-end process.

- It would have been helpful to determine the appropriate sample sizes and factor in typical response rates. The data collection plan also should have identified the sales codes affiliated with each program. These codes are used in the systems that capture revenue projections and results. There were adjustments in the delivery phase that could have reinforced the expected business results and improved completion of evaluations. Ideally, the evaluation planning should have been communicated to students during the instructor-led portion of the event. Additionally, the action plans could have been more fully integrated into the course activities.

- Scorecards serve varied audiences and multiple purposes. Sponsoring stakeholders and business leaders can discern the effects of training through high-level summaries. Training executives and internal training teams can use snapshot views of training effectiveness for internal program modifications and refinements. Students and their supervising managers can be more active in the training process. Supporting the philosophical move from training as entitlement to training is a means to help enhance overall business performance.

- Scorecard metrics must be credible and reliable to be used effectively. It is critical to articulate and validate assumptions, especially with a synopsis-style scorecard. The scorecard documentation should articulate data collection methodology and information sources clearly. Internal stakeholders need to be engaged in the formative stages of scorecard development to ensure their support and validation upon its publication. Another critical aspect of scorecard development and production is ensuring the use of conservative estimates to derive results. In order to maintain credibility with the business, it is better to understate rather than overstate the business impact of training. Often, the data will be collected from areas and systems outside the training organization's direct influence. As a result, it is important for the data analysts within the training organization to understand the data.

- In this example, an executive chain of command, including senior training leaders and senior members of the sponsoring organization, provided the communication mechanism for reporting results. Executive involvement enhanced perceived value and integrity of the scorecard results. After the initial surprise that these metrics have been compiled, the business leaders tended to look for "holes" in the metrics. The clearly defined assumptions were invaluable in producing credible results. One key aspect in the timing of these scorecard readouts was to ensure that the report frequency was timely with respect to meeting the leaders' needs for this information. Timing that should be defined consistently for all reports—initial, interim, and, if appropriate, final. Communication with trainees and their supervising managers should have included expectations of participation and the purpose of the evaluations. Ideally, students should have been advised of the times at which to expect surveys and other mechanisms for capturing results. Program results reporting relied solely on individual performance results captured from the sales funnel systems. It would have been more powerful to include student and manager input to further validate results, such as action plans.

- The trend analysis was extremely helpful in boosting the credibility of the comparison group. One interpretation was that other influences were contributing factors; both training participants and nonparticipants experienced an increase in lead performance around the sales initiative launch. Regardless of these influences, the training participants had a higher lead performance than their nontraining counterparts. Acknowledging additional influence on account executive lead performance and isolating the impact of the training program were critical in building credibility with the senior sales leaders.

- The initial executive summaries included too much information. These reports were more useful for internal training teams' assessing the cost efficiency and effectiveness of each delivery mode. For the executives, simply focusing on one aspect of the program, such as the instructor-led portion, proved most effective. This type of information generated discussion between the senior sales leaders and the senior training leaders. At times, secondary analyses were requested to explore or validate the original analysis.

- The major success of this learning program was its ability to impact the bottom line. The exceptional success for this training organization was the ability to prove it. Key factors in this success included executive partnership between the senior sales and training leaders and executive sponsorship from the LS vice president. The use of these results to spur additional discussion between these groups on an ongoing basis was an additional win for both organizations and the business. Internally, the training organization has used the measurement efforts surrounding this program as a model for ongoing efforts and a tool for cultural transformation. These results have continued to reinforce the criticality of training alignment with business priorities.

- These measurement efforts have been expanded to other programs. Many of the lessons learned have been incorporated into new processes and an iterative methodology for measuring training. The measurement outputs continue to be simple, one-page graphic views, which remain extremely effective with various audiences. The business impact data is still the focus of these reports, although ROI data is collected for support. The overall strategy is to focus on the business impact of programs and curricula. The goal of the ROI is to exceed the total investment in training through the value produced in the major, strategic programs and curricula. At the end of the year, the vice president of training wants to be able to assert that each

$1 spent on training contributed $1+ to the bottom line. The team aspires to continue affecting the bottom line positively, demonstrating the value of training, and using this information to optimize training investments to create a best-in-class training organization that supports a growing and profitable business.

## Questions for Discussion

1.  Why is the evaluation and data planning phase important? How does an organization effectively incorporate this type of planning into training design?
2.  How can training begin to identify valid indicators of future performance or results using current workforce information (for example, workforce profiles, skills inventories, and certifications)?
3.  How can these types of results be combined to provide a more holistic, systematic view of training impact?
4.  Regarding the communication of results, how do you identify the right stakeholders, level of detail, and frequency?
5.  How do you capture lessons learned? With whom do you share these lessons? How does sharing these lessons improve your effectiveness and ability to preempt challenges?

## The Authors

Stephanie Barber is the program manager for LS's quarterly scorecard. She has been involved in HR measurement for several years. She was a program manager for Saratoga OnLine, a team member on the Balanced Scorecard Collaborative Action Working Group for Human Resources, and a representative for the Ford Attrition Consortium. Prior to her current position, she managed the corporation-wide production of monthly workforce results and general workforce analysis. Barber received her bachelor of arts degree in psychology and sociology from the State University of New York, and a master of arts degree in industrial psychology and a master's degree in business administration/human resource management from Fairleigh Dickinson University. She has achieved Franklin Covey Return-on-Investment certification status. She can be reached at 908.658.0699.

Patricia Albaugh is a program manager currently responsible for accreditation and certification planning and design for the sales organization. She has been involved in corporate education in all phases, from needs assessment through development and delivery to evaluation. She received her bachelor of science degree in business administration from State University College at Oswego and is pursuing her master's degree in information resource management at Syracuse University. Albaugh has achieved Franklin Covey Return-on-Investment certification status and is a member of ASTD and the ROI Network.

## References

Kaplan, Robert S., and David P. Norton. (1996). *The Balanced Scorecard: Translating Strategy into Action.* Boston: Harvard Business School Press.

Kirkpatrick, Donald L. (1998). *Evaluating Training Programs: The Four Levels.* 2nd ed. San Francisco: Berrett-Koehler.

Phillips, Jack J. (1997). *Handbook of Training Evaluation and Measurement Methods: Proven Models and Methods of Evaluating Any HRD Program.* 3rd ed. Boston: Butterworth-Heinemann.

# Caterpillar University Dashboard: Measuring—and Maximizing— the Business Value of Learning

## Caterpillar, Inc.

### Merrill C. Anderson and Chris Arvin

*Caterpillar recently established a corporate university to achieve the vision of becoming a true continual learning organization that embraces employees, dealers, suppliers, and customers. Colleges within the university were established to focus on specific learning areas and to better leverage learning and knowledge management across the business enterprise. Governance bodies were established to develop learning strategies and provide oversight of Caterpillar University and its component colleges. The Caterpillar University performance dashboard was created to capture the business value of learning and to provide insights into how best to manage the university as a strategic asset for the business.*

## The Strategic Role of Learning at Caterpillar

Caterpillar, Inc., is the world's leading manufacturer of heavy construction equipment, offering customers 24 machine families. Caterpillar dealers around the globe are supported by more than 2,000 parts distribution facilities to ensure efficient postsale customer service. Building on more than 75 years of success, Caterpillar has embarked on an aggressive growth strategy that will increase annual revenue to $30 billion from $20 billion. Continual learning and continuous improvement were recognized by Caterpillar leaders as essential ingredients to achieving their growth strategy. Caterpillar University was established in 2001 to accelerate both continual learning and, in conjunction with the Six Sigma effort, to help create an environment of continuous improvement.

*This case was prepared to serve as a basis for discussion rather than to illustrate either effective or ineffective administrative and management practices.*

The president of Caterpillar University and his team have described building a continual learning organization as a journey (figure 1). This journey began by focusing on a series of business enterprise learning initiatives. Six Sigma was initiated and Caterpillar University provided leadership in facilitating Six Sigma training. Caterpillar University launched initiatives to build leadership bench strength, including a new competency model, in-depth assessments, coaching, and other leadership activities. E-learning was accelerated and aggressive goals were set to appropriately replace classroom-delivered training with e-learning. The Knowledge Network was established and quickly grew to more than 1,000 communities that shared best practices, ideas, tools, processes, and specifications and that quickly solved vexing problems.

Caterpillar University also created efficiencies and increased the quality of learning development and delivery. Learning best practices from around the world were initiated. Common learning processes and methodologies were identified. A performance consulting model, for example, was explained to the global learning managers and deployment was initiated. A common needs assessment process was implemented to show where learning was needed to achieve business goals. State-of-the-art learning evaluation practices were communicated worldwide. These evaluation practices included developing a learning performance dashboard and conducting specific evaluation studies on learning initiatives.

## Caterpillar University: Vision and Mission, Structure, and Governance

The vision of Caterpillar University is "to be recognized as a highly valued, professional group, leading the company's learning effort in a fun, exciting, and caring atmosphere." Its mission extends its learning solutions across the value chain to "improve the performance of Caterpillar employees, dealers, suppliers, and customers." The university is well positioned to enable the business enterprise to achieve its learning vision of being "recognized as one of the best continual learning organizations in the world."

To achieve the vision and mission of continual learning, the university was organized into a series of colleges, each dedicated to a strategic learning area and each address the entire business enterprise and value chain. These colleges are
• business and business processes
• dealers, customers, and markets
• dealer technical training

# Figure 1. The journey: building a continual learning organization.

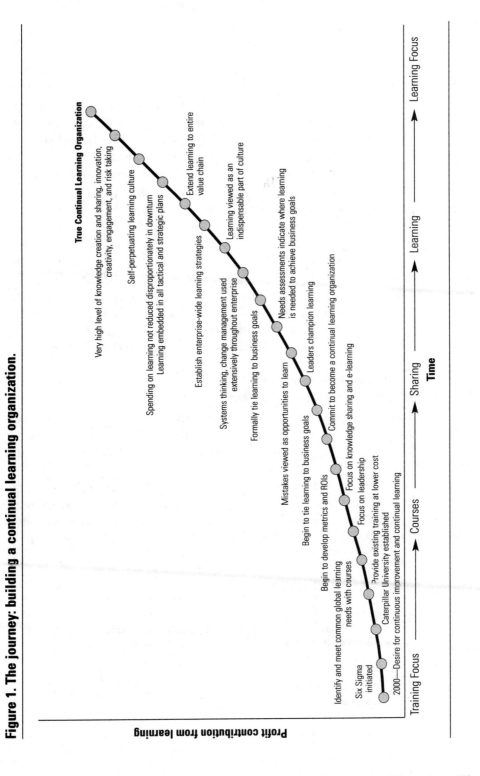

True Continual Learning Organization

Very high level of knowledge creation and sharing, innovation,
creativity, engagement, and risk taking

Self-perpetuating learning culture

Spending on learning not reduced disproportionately in downturn
Learning embedded in all tactical and strategic plans

Extend learning to entire
value chain

Establish enterprise-wide learning strategies

Learning viewed as an
indispensable part of culture

Systems thinking, change management used
extensively throughout enterprise

Needs assessments indicate where learning
is needed to achieve business goals

Formally tie learning to business goals

Leaders champion learning

Mistakes viewed as opportunities to learn

Commit to become a continual learning organization

Begin to tie learning to business goals

Focus on knowledge sharing and e-learning

Begin to develop metrics and ROIs

Focus on leadership

Identify and meet common global learning
needs with courses

Provide existing training at lower cost

Caterpillar University established

Six Sigma
initiated

2000—Desire for continuous improvement and continual learning

Profit contribution from learning

Training Focus ⟶ Courses ⟶ Sharing ⟶ Learning ⟶ Learning Focus

Time

- general studies
- leadership
- technology
- Six Sigma.

Given the scope and breadth of the corporate university, effective governance was viewed as critical for success. Two primary types of governance bodies were established (figure 2). The board of governors was established to provide oversight of the entire learning capability for Caterpillar. Included on this board were the CEO and several senior business and functional leaders. The president of Caterpillar University served as the chairman of the board and queued up strategic issues and decisions for the board's quarterly meetings.

The second type of governance body was the advisory board—one for each college. Membership included senior leaders from the user groups of the respective colleges. These boards set priorities for the colleges and ensured that user perspectives were given a voice in developing and deploying learning. Both the board of governors and the advisory boards were effective mechanisms for increasing leadership understanding and commitment to continual learning.

## Training Dashboard Methodology
### The Caterpillar University Dashboard: Measuring the Business Value

Regular measurement and management of learning performance was considered essential to realizing the vision of becoming a continual learning organization. The president of Caterpillar University decided to develop a learning performance dashboard that would enable better management of learning and support the decision making of the board of governors regarding the development and implementation of learning strategy. Caterpillar, Inc., did not have a formal performance scorecard. Instead, the corporation identified

**Figure 2. Caterpillar University governance.**

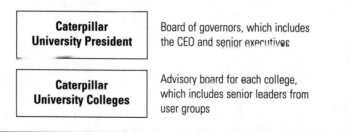

a set of critical success factors for the business. Caterpillar University initiatives were launched in support of these critical success factors and it was intended that the performance of these initiatives be tracked using the dashboard. Figure 3 presents the entire dashboard.

Following a rapid prototyping model, a future-state dashboard was designed based on what the university learning leaders considered to be essential learning performance information. The current-state model was developed during the prototyping. Both the current state and the desired state of the learning performance dashboard were presented to the first board of governors meeting.

### Using Rapid Prototyping to Develop the Dashboard

A sponsor for learning evaluation was identified within Caterpillar University, and this person worked with internal and external resources to advance the scorecard concept. A four-step process based on rapid prototyping principles was used to quickly develop the dashboard quickly. Following are the steps used.

1. *Develop a straw-model dashboard.* With the intention of "starting with the answer in mind," the first step in this process was to develop a straw-model, or prototype, dashboard that incorporated best practices in learning and evaluation. Best practices indicated that the dashboard should consist of three major elements: budget performance, volume measurement, and learning levels evaluation. This straw model was viewed as a starting point that would undergo several enhancements.

2. *Enhance the straw model through internal review.* The dashboard was reviewed by several people inside Caterpillar University and was enhanced based on the feedback received. Decisions were made about several issues, including the following:

   a. *How detailed should the dashboard be?* The intention was to keep the dashboard to one page and to entertain breakouts by business units at a later time. The defined purposes of the dashboard were to highlight potential issues (and successes!) and to stimulate appropriate investigations (but not to contain the detailed information needed for those investigations).

   b. *How frequently should the dashboard data be compiled and reviewed?* The decision was to do this on a quarterly rather than a monthly basis, in part because the systems to produce the data were not yet automated.

   c. *Should period (for example, quarterly) data be presented with YTD data?* In the interest of simplicity, period data would not be included in the dashboard.

# Figure 3. Corporate University continual learning dashboard.

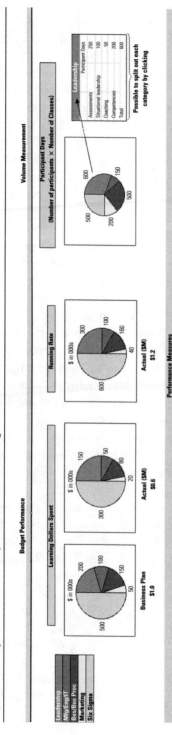

**Budget Performance**

**Volume Measurement**

**Learning Dollars Spent** — Business Plan $1.0, Actual ($M) $0.6

**Running Rate** — Actual ($M) $1.2

**Participant Days** (Number of participants × Number of Classes)

| Leadership | Participant Days |
| --- | --- |
| Assessments | 250 |
| Situational leadership | 100 |
| Coaching | 50 |
| Competencies | 200 |
| Total | 600 |

Possible to split out each category by clicking

**Performance Measures**

### Level I: Reaction

| | Percent of Courses Assessed | | | Percent Favorable | | |
| --- | --- | --- | --- | --- | --- | --- |
| | Target | Actual | % Diff | Target | Actual | % Diff |
| Leadership | 95% | 75% | -19% | 85% | 91% | 6% |
| Mfg/Eng/IT | 95% | 91% | -3% | 85% | 78% | -7% |
| Bus/Bus Proc | 95% | 88% | -10% | 85% | 87% | 2% |
| Marketing | 95% | 91% | -4% | 85% | 81% | -4% |
| Six Sigma | 95% | 99% | 3% | 85% | 72% | -13% |
| Total | 95% | 88% | -7% | 85% | 82% | -3% |

### Level II: Comprehension

| | Percent of Courses Assessed | | | Average Test Score | | |
| --- | --- | --- | --- | --- | --- | --- |
| | Target | Actual | % Diff | Target | Actual | % Diff |
| Leadership | 40% | 38% | -2% | 80% | 82% | 2% |
| Mfg/Eng/IT | 40% | 62% | 22% | 80% | 64% | -16% |
| Bus/Bus Proc | 40% | 28% | -12% | 80% | 77% | -3% |
| Marketing | 40% | 56% | 16% | 80% | 68% | -12% |
| Six Sigma | 40% | 95% | 55% | 80% | 87% | 7% |
| Total | 40% | 56% | 16% | 80% | 76% | -4% |

### Level III: Application

| | Percent of Courses Assessed | | | Percent Application | | |
| --- | --- | --- | --- | --- | --- | --- |
| | Target | Actual | % Diff | Target | Actual | % Diff |
| Leadership | 20% | 18% | -2% | 70% | 57% | -13% |
| Mfg/Eng/IT | 20% | 27% | 7% | 70% | 64% | -6% |
| Bus/Bus Proc | 20% | 39% | 19% | 70% | 80% | 10% |
| Marketing | 20% | 15% | -5% | 70% | 46% | -24% |
| Six Sigma | 20% | 95% | 75% | 70% | 95% | 25% |
| Total | 20% | 39% | 19% | 70% | 68% | -2% |

### Level IV: Business Results

| | Percent of Courses Assessed | | | Accumulated Dollars (000s) | | |
| --- | --- | --- | --- | --- | --- | --- |
| | Target | Actual | % Diff | Target | Actual | $ Diff |
| Leadership | 5% | 15% | 10% | 250 | 300 | 50 |
| Mfg/Eng/IT | 5% | 0% | -5% | 75 | 100 | 25 |
| Bus/Bus Proc | 5% | 0% | -5% | 130 | 160 | 30 |
| Marketing | 5% | 9% | 4% | 2,500 | 40 | (2,460) |
| Six Sigma | 5% | 0% | -5% | 550 | 600 | 50 |
| Total | 5% | 3% | -2% | 3,505 | 1,200 | (2,305) |

### Level V: ROI

| | Percent of Courses Assessed | | | ROI Percentage | | |
| --- | --- | --- | --- | --- | --- | --- |
| | Target | Actual | % Diff | Target | Actual | % Diff |
| Leadership | 5% | 15% | 10% | 10% | 12% | 2% |
| Mfg/Eng/IT | 5% | 0% | -5% | 20% | 28% | 8% |
| Bus/Bus Proc | 5% | 0% | -5% | 15% | 18% | 3% |
| Marketing | 5% | 9% | 4% | 100% | 2% | -98% |
| Six Sigma | 5% | 0% | -5% | 100% | 108% | 8% |
| Total | 5% | 3% | -2% | 49% | 34% | -15% |

**Notes**

d. *Should "percent of courses" or "percent of participants" be the unit of assessment?* The decision was to begin with the percent of courses being assessed—a choice that relieved some of the burden of data collection. When the worldwide implementation of the learning management system was complete, this and other dashboard decisions could be reconsidered.

3. *Present the dashboard to the board of governors.* This dashboard, along with current state learning metrics, was presented to the board of governors. The board was very impressed with how Caterpillar University was being run as an efficient business, endorsed the notion of evaluating the business value of learning, and offered specific ideas about what learning initiatives to consider.

4. *Deploy the dashboard, making refinements as required.* The prototype dashboard was viewed as a beginning. Data would be compiled over a period of time, beginning first with the data at the top of the dashboard and then working down the document. Worldwide deployment of the learning management system was considered essential to compile Levels 1–5 data efficiently.

## Guidelines for Learning Evaluation Methodology

University leadership identified 10 guidelines for learning evaluation methodology to support achieving the vision of becoming a continual learning organization. These guidelines are intended to support the continuing development of the dashboard and to support decision making about learning and development.

1. *Learning goals are tied to business goals, so that measuring learning is also measuring an aspect of business performance.* In a continual learning organization, there is no meaningful distinction between learning and working.

2. *Issues with learning performance are viewed as opportunities to improve the effectiveness and business value of learning.* Continuous improvement is impossible without first understanding what opportunities exist to make improvements. Evaluating learning is essential to understand what these opportunities are and how best to improve them.

3. *All learning strategies will have an evaluation component.* Learning objectives for each learning initiative will be linked to the appropriate evaluation objectives and will be supportive of achieving business goals. Not all learning (in fact, only a small fraction) will be evaluated at Level 4 or Level 5. However, the evaluation level selected will correspond to the level of learning expected. A learning initiative that sets its learning goal at the application level, for example, will be evaluated at Level 3.

4. *Running learning and development functions as an efficient and effective business requires sound performance measurement.* Learning and development initiatives compete for investment dollars with other business initiatives. Learning produces real business value, but learning performance measurement is essential to show how learning will create that value and to compete effectively for funding with other investment options.

5. *A learning performance dashboard will be maintained and regularly reviewed by learning leaders and governing bodies to highlight successes and indicate potential performance issues.* The quality and impact of decisions regarding learning strategies and deployment of learning initiatives are greatly enhanced when they are based on facts and on reliable learning performance data. When root causes of performance issues can be identified and addressed more readily, learning performance—and business performance—are improved.

6. *Whenever possible, consistent and common learning evaluation tools will be developed and used worldwide.* Implementing a dashboard can be a major leverage point for driving consistency of learning development and delivery worldwide. A common approach to Level 1 evaluation, for example, enables cross-business enterprise comparisons. Greater consistency will drive down the cost of learning as processes are developed once (and only once) and then are implemented worldwide.

7. *Learning will be evaluated at five levels, with minimum percentage thresholds of courses evaluated at each level.* The learning governance bodies will establish these threshold percentages and change them over time to best meet learning and business needs. Intangible benefits also will be noted as appropriate.

8. *Determining the financial return-on-investment (ROI) will be performed only on those learning initiatives that are large in scope and strategic in nature.* The intention is to select only those learning initiatives that are expected to have a significant business impact. Business and learning leaders decide which initiatives to evaluate at Level 5, with a clear idea about the potential impact that the initiative likely will have on the business.

9. *Learning evaluation processes and tools will be consistent with Six Sigma and, when appropriate, integrated into Six Sigma processes.* Six Sigma is a major process initiative to make continuous improvement a standard business practice. Continuous improvement and continual learning are mutually dependent, and both are required for Caterpillar to reach its business goal of becoming a $30 billion-revenue company.

10. *Assessing the job performance of individual learning leaders will be based in part on achieving learning performance targets.* Caterpillar has set some aggressive business and learning goals. Holding learning leaders

accountable for reaching their goals and meeting their commitments to the business is essential. Learning metrics enable specific, measurable performance targets to be set for learning leaders, and they clearly indicate whether these targets have been met.

## Training Dashboard Application

The dashboard consists of three major elements: budget performance, volume measurement, and learning levels evaluation. Each of these elements will be described in detail along with examples of how the data can be used not only to measure learning performance, but also to better *manage* learning performance.

### Budget Performance

Budget performance was captured by the categories of learning dollars spent and benefit dollars accumulated for five of the major colleges (figure 4). This data is cumulative for each fiscal year. Learning dollars planned to be spent versus dollars actually spent indicates, on a quarterly basis, how learning investments are being made by each college. Learning initiatives that produce documented dollar benefits have these benefits accumulated each quarter. Business and learning leaders quickly are able to compare dollars spent with dollars returned as benefits by each college. This comparison allows the board of governors to establish specific budget performance expectations for each college as well as for the university overall. As shown in figure 4, for example, Caterpillar University has spent $600,000 from a plan of $1 million. The accumulated dollars from all five colleges show benefits of $1.2 million. (This is fictitious data, as is all scorecard data, and is intended for illustrative purposes only.)

## Figure 4. Budget performance.

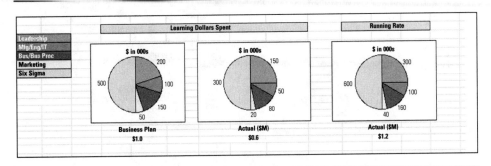

## Volume Measurement

The volume of learning and development performance was captured as participant days (figure 5). A participant day was determined by multiplying the number of participants by the number of classroom days. This was calculated for each major college and for the university overall. Breakouts for each college indicate the participant days metric for major programs of that given college. This information reveals where the budget dollars are being spent and how the learning priorities are being met on a program-by-program basis. The example in figure 5 shows a total of 600 participant days for leadership development out of a total of 1,950 participant days from all five colleges. The breakout examination shows the participant days for specific leadership initiatives.

## Learning Levels Evaluation

One of the learning evaluation principles (described later in this case study) stipulated that all learning initiatives have an evaluation component. This evaluation is conducted along the lines suggested by Kirkpatrick (1977) and Phillips (1997):

- Level 1: Reaction of the participants to the learning
- Level 2: Comprehension of the learning material
- Level 3: Application of what participants learned
- Level 4: Financial results resulting from the application of the learning
- Level 5: The ROI generated by the learning initiative.

**Figure 5. Volume measurement.**

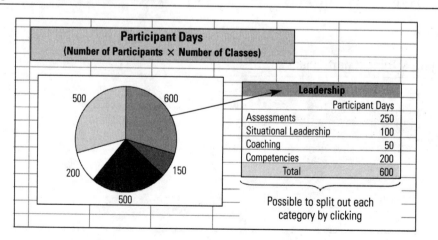

It is intended that the evaluation plan of each learning initiative be linked to the learning objectives. This means that not every learning initiative will be evaluated according to all five evaluation levels—in fact, very few (5 percent) learning initiatives will be evaluated at all five levels (refer to learning evaluation principles later in this case study).

According to the dashboard, each of the major colleges has evaluations summarized for Levels 1 through 5. It is intended that Level 1 reaction and Level 2 comprehension (figure 6) performance data be summarized in terms of the percent of courses assessed at each level and the percent favorable. This data in figure 6 is presented for each major college. Target percentages are shown for each level and college and can be compared with the actual percentages achieved. The percentage difference shows the extent to which performance exceeds the target (a positive percentage) or falls short (a negative percentage).

**Figure 6. Levels 1 and 2 measurements.**

| | Level I: Reaction | | | | | |
|---|---|---|---|---|---|---|
| | Percent of Courses Assessed | | | Percent Favorable | | |
| | Target | Actual | % Diff | Target | Actual | % Diff |
| Leadership | 95% | 76% | −19% | 85% | 91% | 6% |
| Mfg/Eng/IT | 95% | 92% | −3% | 85% | 78% | −7% |
| Bus/Bus Proc | 95% | 85% | −10% | 85% | 87% | 2% |
| Marketing | 95% | 91% | −4% | 85% | 81% | −4% |
| Six Sigma | 95% | 98% | 3% | 85% | 72% | −13% |
| Total | 95% | 88% | −7% | 85% | 82% | −3% |

| | Level II: Comprehension | | | | | |
|---|---|---|---|---|---|---|
| | Percent of Courses Assessed | | | Average Test Score | | |
| | Target | Actual | % Diff | Target | Actual | % Diff |
| Leadership | 40% | 38% | −2% | 80% | 82% | 2% |
| Mfg/Eng/IT | 40% | 62% | 22% | 80% | 64% | −16% |
| Bus/Bus Proc | 40% | 28% | −12% | 80% | 77% | −3% |
| Marketing | 40% | 56% | 16% | 80% | 68% | −12% |
| Six Sigma | 40% | 95% | 55% | 80% | 87% | 7% |
| Total | 40% | 56% | 16% | 80% | 76% | −4% |

Examining the (fictitious) data in figure 6, for example, reveals that the reactions of participants to manufacturing/engineering/IT initiatives as well as to Six Sigma training are below target levels. In this illustration, the data may indicate a need for some further investigation. In looking at the Level 2 comprehension data, however, the Six Sigma training test scores are above target. This is especially impressive given that 95 percent of the Six Sigma courses were assessed at this level. The test scores for manufacturing/engineering/IT, however, tell a different story. Average test scores for these learning initiatives were 16 percent below target. Given the Level 1 evaluation performance, it certainly would be appropriate to investigate the performance of these initiatives and make any needed corrective actions. The 68 percent average test score for marketing initiatives also bears watching closely. The Level 1 scores are about at target level, but being generally satisfied with the learning environment does not necessarily mean that people are learning in that environment.

Level 3 application (figure 7) performance is addressed in the dashboard in terms of the percentage of courses assessed at this level and the percentage of courses that include an application component. Again, for purposes of illustration, these percentages are presented for each major college and offer target versus actual performance comparisons. When looking at the data in figure 7, the overall performance for Caterpillar University appears to be on target. The percentage of

**Figure 7. Level 3 measurement.**

| Level III: Application | | | | | |
|---|---|---|---|---|---|
| **Percent of Courses Assessed** | | | **Percent Application** | | |
| Target | Actual | % Diff | Target | Actual | % Diff |
| Leadership | 20% | 18% | −2% | 70% | 57% | −13% |
| Mfg/Eng/IT | 20% | 27% | 7% | 70% | 64% | −6% |
| Bus/Bus Proc | 20% | 39% | 19% | 70% | 80% | 10% |
| Marketing | 20% | 15% | −5% | 70% | 46% | −24% |
| Six Sigma | 20% | 95% | 75% | 70% | 95% | 25% |
| Total | 20% | 39% | 19% | 70% | 68% | −2% |

courses assessed is running 19 percent above target and the percent of participants applying course material to the workplace is very close to target (-2 percent). Examining the results of each college, however, reveals some issues that must be addressed. Application of learning from marketing courses, for example, is 24 percent below target. If sales people are not adequately applying what they have learned, it is doubtful that they will produce the increased revenue that business leaders are expecting. Immediate action is required to address this issue.

Level 4 business results and Level 5 ROI sections (figure 8) complete the dashboard. It is intended that the Level 4 data shows, for each college, the percentage of courses assessed at this level and the benefit dollars that have been accumulated. The actual benefit dollars achieved can be compared with targets to show differences. Because this data is compiled quarterly and accumulated on an annual basis, differences in the early part of the year are likely to be negative and then to become increasingly more positive throughout the year as benefit dollars are accumulated. Level 5 ROI percentages are calculated for programs in each college by the following equation:

$$ROI = ([benefits - costs]/costs) \times 100$$

The intention for this dashboard is to display target versus actual ROI performance for each college. It is important to note that, according to best practices, ROI data is drawn from only a fraction (for example, about 5 percent) of the learning initiatives. For purposes of illustration, examining the data from figure 8 shows that with the exception of marketing, all colleges are delivering the expected business results. For marketing it may be too early to realize these benefits because there is a time lag between completing a sales course and producing increased revenue based on what was learned in that sales course. However, given the previously noted sub-par Level 3 application performance, it would be worthwhile to investigate this issue further.

## Communicating Results

The initial draft of the dashboard was presented to the board of governors. The presentation was intended to familiarize the board with learning evaluation methodology and to receive specific direction on evaluating learning programs. The board indicated that it was

**Figure 8. Levels 4 and 5 measurements.**

| Level IV: Business Results | | | | | | |
|---|---|---|---|---|---|---|
| | Percent of Courses Assessed | | | Accumulated Dollars (000s) | | |
| | Target | Actual | % Diff | Target | Actual | % Diff |
| Leadership | 5% | 15% | 10% | 250 | 300 | 50 |
| Mfg/Eng/IT | 5% | 0% | -5% | 75 | 100 | 25 |
| Bus/Bus Proc | 5% | 0% | -5% | 130 | 160 | 30 |
| Marketing | 5% | 9% | 4% | 2,500 | 40 | (2,460) |
| Six Sigma | 5% | 0% | -5% | 550 | 600 | 50 |
| Total | 5% | 3% | -2% | 3,505 | 1,200 | (2,305) |

| Level V: ROI | | | | | | |
|---|---|---|---|---|---|---|
| | Percent of Courses Assessed | | | ROI Percentage | | |
| | Target | Actual | % Diff | Target | Actual | % Diff |
| Leadership | 5% | 15% | 10% | 10% | 12% | 2% |
| Mfg/Eng/IT | 5% | 0% | -5% | 20% | 28% | 8% |
| Bus/Bus Proc | 5% | 0% | -5% | 15% | 18% | 3% |
| Marketing | 5% | 9% | 4% | 100% | 2% | -98% |
| Six Sigma | 5% | 0% | -5% | 100% | 108% | 8% |
| Total | 5% | 3% | -2% | 49% | 34% | -15% |

most interested in budget performance and in how Caterpillar University was providing a financial ROI. The board indicated that it would most like to see ROI studies performed on learning programs that directly affect the core business. Three learning programs were selected: Web-based training for assemblers, the Knowledge Network, and training for sales representatives. These studies were conducted, and the results were discussed at the next quarterly board meeting.

The dashboard also was presented to the global learning managers' meeting, which was hosted by Caterpillar University. More than 70 meeting participants from around the world gathered to set the annual agenda for learning and development programs. The dashboard was presented in the context of learning evaluation methodology. Global learning managers had varying degrees of knowledge about learning evaluation. Two educational efforts were launched. First, a Web-based training on learning evaluation was created to enhance the overall level of knowledge about learning evaluation. Being Web-based enabled this learning application to be accessed by people around the world. Second, a learning evaluation community of practice was initiated to provide a virtual way for people to discuss evaluation issues, address questions, and communicate evaluation-related information worldwide.

## Lessons Learned

Experts in learning technology within Caterpillar University embarked on an effort to document learning volume measurements based on available data. The lessons learned from this effort offered a sobering assessment of how quickly the prototype dashboard could be implemented effectively. These learnings included the following:

- Data is kept in a variety of systems, often requiring hand tabulation. It was clear that many of the questions regarding learning performance had not been asked before or in such a detailed way. Consequently, there was no consistent system for gathering even the most basic data, for example, participant days.
- Data collection procedures were not consistently applied. Data was gathered in different ways by different groups, often with varying definitions for data categories, for example, what constitutes a "course."
- Much of the data required validation. The variation in data collection procedures led to an apples-and-oranges comparison of data, and that required the person organizing the data to communicate with the data providers and validate what was submitted.
- Decision rules were needed for comparing classroom learning and e-learning. The intention of e-learning is to be a continuous source of improving performance. Classroom delivery, on the other hand, provides discrete concentrations of learning on a particular topic. Entering both kinds of performance data into common categories requires decision rules about how to put these two delivery methods on an even footing.
- Including dealers and suppliers added another level of complexity. A major expected contribution of Caterpillar University, and of learning in general, is to create business benefits throughout the value chain. Recordkeeping and learning performance disciplines vary a

great deal among dealers, and gaining greater consistency in their learning processes will be required to include their data in the dashboard.

## Questions for Discussion

1. What is the distinction between a dashboard and a scorecard, and how might both tools be used together to better manage learning performance?
2. How can dashboard data be used to set the agenda for the corporate university's board of governors?
3. What additional measurement elements could be added to the dashboard and what would these elements tell you?
4. How do you determine what the optimum frequency of reporting is for a performance dashboard—weekly, monthly, quarterly? What are the implications for decision making?
5. How can dashboard data be used to enhance the implementation of learning strategy?

## The Authors

Merrill C. Anderson, the chief executive officer of MetrixGlobal, LLC, has worked with more than 100 companies in North America and Europe to manage strategic organization change effectively. He has more than 30 professional publications and speeches to his credit, including the books *Strategic Change: Fast Cycle Organization Development* and *Building Learning Capability Through Outsourcing*. Anderson currently is clinical professor in education at Drake University and was recently elected to the ASTD ROI Advisory Council. He earned his doctorate at New York University. He can be reached at merrilland@metrixglobal.net.

Chris Arvin is the dean of leadership for Caterpillar University. The university was established formally in 2001 to help Caterpillar, Inc., become a continual learning organization. Arvin has worked for 10 years at Caterpillar, primarily in the financial arena, and recently has accepted the challenge to develop the corporation's common global framework for leadership development. Most recently, he was the profit center manager for the Europe, Africa, and Middle East marketing operation located in Geneva, Switzerland. Prior to joining Caterpillar, he worked as a certified public accountant for Arthur Andersen & Co. in the Chicago office.

# References

Kirkpatrick, Donald L. (1977). "Evaluating Training Programs: Evidence vs. Proof." *Training and Development Journal*, 31: 9-12.

Phillips, Jack J. (1997). *Return on Investment in Training and Performance Programs*. Boston: Butterworth-Heinemann.

# About the Editor

Lynn Schmidt is the director of the Leadership Institute at Nextel Communications. She has 17 years of experience as a human and organization development professional in the fast-paced high-technology industry. In her current position she is responsible for succession management, identification and development of high-potential candidates, diversity and mentoring programs, and executive development. Schmidt also has had responsibility for performance consulting, management and employee training curricula, new employee integration, distance learning, instructional systems design, competency modeling, and employee satisfaction surveys.

Schmidt has extensive experience in the field of measurement and evaluation. She is certified in ROI evaluation and was president-elect for the ROI Network. She currently serves on the ASTD ROI Network Advisory Committee. In 2002 she received the Jack and Patti Phillips ROI Practitioner of the Year Award. Schmidt authored a case study on evaluating soft-skills training for ASTD's *In Action* series book *Measuring Learning and Performance.* She has conducted several ROI/impact studies on programs such as change management, time management, performance management, and diversity awareness.

Schmidt has made presentations on measurement and evaluation at several conferences sponsored by the International Quality and Productivity Center, ASTD, and the ROI Network. She teaches both needs assessment and measurement and evaluation at Georgetown University. She serves as co-director of programs for the Metro D.C. ASTD chapter and was a member of the 2001 and 2002 ASTD program committees for the annual ASTD international conference. She holds a bachelor of science degree in business administration, a master's of business administration, and is pursuing a doctorate in human and organization development. Schmidt can be reached at lynn.schmidt@nextel.com or at 703.433.4524.

# About the Series Editor

Jack J. Phillips is a world-renowned expert on measurement and evaluation and developer of the ROI Process, a revolutionary process that provides bottom-line figures and accountability for all types of training, performance improvement, human resources, and technology programs. He is the author or editor of more than 30 books—12 focused on measurement and evaluation—and more than 100 articles.

His expertise in measurement and evaluation is based on more than 27 years of corporate experience in five industries (aerospace, textiles, metals, construction materials, and banking). Phillips has served as training and development manager at two *Fortune* 500 firms, senior HR officer at two firms, president of a regional federal savings bank, and management professor at a major state university.

In 1992, Phillips founded Performance Resources Organization (PRO), an international consulting firm that provides comprehensive assessment, measurement, and evaluation services for organizations. In 1999, PRO was acquired by the Franklin Covey Company and is now known as The Jack Phillips Center for Research. Today the center is an independent leading provider of measurement and evaluation services to the global business community. Phillips consults with clients in manufacturing, service, and government organizations in the United States, Canada, Sweden, England, Belgium, Germany, Italy, Holland, South Africa, Mexico, Venezuela, Malaysia, Indonesia, Hong Kong, Australia, New Zealand, and Singapore. Phillips leads the center's research and publishing efforts that support the knowledge and development of assessment, measurement, and evaluation.

Books most recently authored by Phillips include *The Human Resources Scorecard: Measuring the Return on Investment*, Butterworth-Heinemann, Boston, MA, 2001; *The Consultant's Scorecard*, McGraw-Hill, New York, NY, 2000; *HRD Trends Worldwide: Shared Solutions to Compete in a Global Economy*, Butterworth-Heinemann, Boston, MA, 1999; *Return on Investment in Training and Performance Improvement Programs*, Butterworth-Heinemann, Boston, MA, 1997; *Handbook of*

*Training Evaluation and Measurement Methods,* 3rd edition, Butterworth-Heinemann, Boston, MA, 1997; and *Accountability in Human Resource Management,* Butterworth-Heinemann, Boston, MA, 1996.

Phillips has undergraduate degrees in electrical engineering, physics, and mathematics from Southern Polytechnic State University and Oglethorpe University, a master's degree in decision sciences from Georgia State University, and a Ph.D. in human resource management from the University of Alabama. In 1987 he won the Yoder-Heneman Personnel Creative Application Award from the Society for Human Resource Management.

Phillips can be reached at The Jack Phillips Center for Research, P.O. Box 380637, Birmingham, AL 35238-0637; phone: 205.678.8038; fax: 205.678.0177; email: serieseditor@aol.com.

# The Value of Belonging

**ASTD membership** keeps you up to date on the latest developments in your field, and provides top-quality, *practical* information to help you stay ahead of trends, polish your skills, measure your progress, demonstrate your effectiveness, and advance your career.

We give you what you need most from the entire scope of workplace learning and performance:

### Information

We're your best resource for research, best practices, and background support materials – the data you need for your projects to excel.

### Networking

We're the facilitator who puts you in touch with colleagues, experts, field specialists, and industry leaders – the people you need to know to succeed.

### Technology

We're the clearinghouse for new technologies in training, learning, and knowledge management in the workplace – the background you need to stay ahead.

### Analysis

We look at cutting-edge practices and programs and give you a balanced view of the latest tools and techniques – the understanding you need on what works and what doesn't.

### Competitive Edge

ASTD is your leading resource on the issues and topics that are important to you. That's the value of belonging!

For more information, or to become a member, please call 1.800.628.2783 (U.S.) or +1.703.683.8100; visit our Website at **www.astd.org**; or send an email to customercare@astd.org.

**ASTD**

*Linking People,
Learning & Performance*

# ASTD PRESS

*Delivering Training and Performance Knowledge*
*You Will Use Today and Lead With Tomorrow*

- Training Basics
- Evaluation and Return-on-Investment (ROI)
- E-Learning
- Instructional Systems Development (ISD)
- Leadership
- Career Development

**ASTD Press** is an internationally renowned source of insightful and practical information on workplace learning and performance topics, including training basics, evaluation and return-on-investment (ROI), instructional systems development (ISD), e-learning, leadership, and career development. You can trust that the books ASTD Press acquires, develops, edits, designs, and publishes meet the highest standards and that they reflect the most current industry practices. In addition, ASTD Press books are bottom-line oriented and geared toward immediate problem-solving application in the field.

**Ordering Information:** Purchase books published by ASTD Press by visiting our Website at store.astd.org or by calling 800.628.2783 or 703.683.8100.

Linking People,
Learning & Performance